C++ Lambda Story

Everything you need to know about Lambda
Expressions in Modern C++!

Bartłomiej Filipek

C++ Lambda Story

Everything you need to know about Lambda Expressions in Modern C++!

Bartłomiej Filipek

for Wiola and Mikołaj

Contents

About the Book

This book shows the story of lambda expressions in C++. You'll learn how to use this powerful feature in a step-by-step manner, slowly digesting the new capabilities and enhancements that come with each revision of the C++ Standard.

We'll start with C++98/03, and then we'll move on to the latest C++ Standards.

- C++98/03 - how to code without lambda support. What was the motivation for the new modern C++ feature?
- C++11 - early days. You'll learn about all the elements of a lambda expression and even some tricks. This is the longest chapter as we need to cover a lot.
- C++14 - updates. Once lambdas were adopted, we saw some options to improve them.
- C++17 - more improvements, especially by handling `this` pointer and allowing `constexpr`.
- C++20 - in this section we'll have a look at the latest and very fresh C++20 Standard.

Additionally, you'll find techniques and handy patterns throughout the chapters for using lambda in your code.

Walking through the evolution of this powerful C++ feature allows us not only to learn lambdas but also to see how C++ has changed over recent years. In one section you'll see a technique and then it will be "iterated" and updated in further chapters when new C++ elements are available. When possible, the book cross-links to other related sections of the book.

Roots Of The Book

The idea for the content started after a live coding presentation given by Tomasz Kamiński at our local Cracow C++ User Group.

I took the ideas from the presentation (with Tomek's permission, of course :) and then created two articles that appeared at bfilipek.com:

- Lambdas: From C++11 to C++20, Part 1[1]
- Lambdas: From C++11 to C++20, Part 2[2]

Later, I decided that I want to offer my readers not only blog posts but a nice-looking PDF. Leanpub provides an easy way to create such PDFs, so it was the right choice to copy the articles' content and create a Leanpub book.

Why not move further?

After some time, I decided to write more content, update the examples, provide better use cases and patterns. And here you have the book! It's now almost **four times** the size of the initial material that is available on the blog!

Who This Book is For

This book is intended for all C++ developers who like to learn all about a modern C++ feature: lambda expressions.

How To Read This Book

This book has the "history" order, so it means that you start from the background behind lambdas, and then you move slowly with new features and capabilities. Reading this book from cover to cover might be suitable for an experienced developer who wants to recall the principles, see the back story and learn what's new in each C++ Standard.

On the other hand, if you are a beginner, it's best to start from the C++11 chapter. See sections about the basic syntax, examples, how to capture variables. Then, when you're ready, you can skip some advanced topics and move into the C++14 chapter where you'll learn about generic lambdas. First parts of the C++11 and C++14 chapter are crucial for understanding lambdas. Once you get the basics, you can read the skipped sections and see more advanced techniques.

At the end of the book in Appendix A, there's a handy list of "lambda techniques". You can have a quick look to see if something is interesting and then start reading that section.

---

[1]https://www.bfilipek.com/2019/02/lambdas-story-part1.html
[2]https://www.bfilipek.com/2019/03/lambdas-story-part2.html

Reader Feedback & Errata

If you spot an error, a typo, a grammar mistake, or anything else (especially logical issues!) that should be corrected, please send your feedback to bartlomiej.filipek AT bfilipek.com.

Here's the errata with the list of fixes:

https://www.cppstories.com/p/cpplambda/

Your feedback matters! If you write an honest review, it can help with the book promotion and the quality of my further work.

If you bought this book through Amazon - as a print or Kindle version - please leave a review there.

What's more, the book has a dedicated page at GoodReads. Please share your feedback:

C++ Lambda Story @GoodReads[3]

Example Code

You can find source code of all examples in this separate Github public repository.

github.com/fenbf/cpplambdastory-code[4]

You can browse individual files or download the whole branch:

github.com/fenbf/cpplambdastory-code/archive/main.zip[5]

Each chapter has its folder, for example, "Lambdas in C++11" has its code in "cpp11".

Each example has a number in the title. For example:

Ex2_3: `std::function` and `auto` type Deduction...

```
// example code...
```

It means that you can go to the second chapter's folder - C++11 and then find the third example. It has the following filename:

`chapter2_cpp11\ex2_3_std_function_and auto.cpp`.

Many examples in the book are relatively short. You can copy and paste the lines into your favourite compiler/IDE and then run the code snippet.

---

[3]https://www.goodreads.com/book/show/53609731-c-lambda-story
[4]https://github.com/fenbf/cpplambdastory-code
[5]https://github.com/fenbf/cpplambdastory-code/archive/main.zip

Code License

The code for the book is available under the Creative Commons License.

Formatting And Special Sections

Code samples are presented in a monospaced font, similar to the following example:

For longer examples:

Title Of the Example

```
#include <iostream>

int main() {
    const std::string text { "Hello World" }
    std::cout << text << '\n';
}
```

Or shorter snippets (without a title and sometimes `include` statements):

```
int foo() {
    return std::clamp(100, 1000, 1001);
}
```

When available, you'll also see a link to the online compiler where you can play with the code. For example:

Example title. Live code @Wandbox

```
#include <iostream>

int main() {
    std::cout << "Hello World!";
}
```

You can click on the link in the title and then it should open the website of a given online compiler (in the above case it's Wandbox). You can compile the sample, see the output and experiment with the code directly in your browser.

Snippets of longer programs were usually shortened to present only the core mechanics.

Syntax Highlighting Limitations

The current version of the book might show some limitations regarding syntax highlighting.

For example:

- `if constexpr` - Link to Pygments issue: C++ if constexpr not recognized (C++17) · Issue #1136[6].
- The first method of a class is not highlighted - First method of class not highlighted in C++ · Issue #791[7].
- Template method is not highlighted C++ lexer doesn't recognize function if return type is templated · Issue #1138[8].
- Modern C++ attributes are sometimes not recognised properly.

Other issues for C++ and Pygments:C++ Issues · github/pygments/pygments[9].

Special Sections

Throughout the book you can also see the following sections:

This is an Information Box, with extra notes related to the current section.

This is a Warning Box with potential risks and threats related to a given topic.

This is a Quote Box. In the book, it's often used to quote the C++ Standard.

---

[6]https://github.com/pygments/pygments/issues/1136
[7]https://github.com/pygments/pygments/issues/791
[8]https://github.com/pygments/pygments/issues/1138
[9]https://github.com/pygments/pygments/issues?q=is%3Aissue+is%3Aopen+C%2B%2B

Online Compilers

Instead of creating local projects to play with the code samples, you can also leverage online compilers. They offer a basic text editor and usually allow you to compile only one source file (the code you edit). They are convenient if you want to play with code samples and check the results using various compilers vendors and versions.

For example, many of the code samples for this book were created using Coliru Online, Wandbox or Compiler Explorer and then adapted for the book.

Here's a list of some of the useful services:

- Coliru[10] - uses GCC 9.2.0 (as of July 2020), offers link sharing and a basic text editor, it's simple but very effective.
- Wandbox[11] - offers a lot of compilers, including most Clang and GCC versions, can use boost libraries; offers link sharing and multiple file compilation.
- Compiler Explorer[12] - offers many compilers, shows generated assembly code, can execute the code, or even make static code analysis.
- CppBench[13] - runs simple C++ performance tests (using google benchmark library).
- BuildBench[14] - allows to compare build times of two C++ programs, shares a similar UI as CppBench.
- C++ Insights[15] - a Clang-based tool for source to source transformation. It shows how the compiler sees the code by expanding lambdas, auto, structured bindings, template deduction, and variadic packs or range-based for loops.

There's also a helpful list of online compilers gathered on this website: List of Online C++ Compilers[16].

---

[10]http://coliru.stacked-crooked.com/
[11]https://wandbox.org/
[12]https://gcc.godbolt.org/
[13]http://quick-bench.com/
[14]https://build-bench.com
[15]https://cppinsights.io/
[16]https://arnemertz.github.io/online-compilers/

About the Author

Bartłomiej (Bartek) Filipek is a C++ software developer from a beautiful city Cracow in Southern Poland. He started his professional career in 2007 and in 2010 he graduated from Jagiellonian University with a Masters Degree in Computer Science.

Bartek currently works at Xara[17], where he develops features for advanced document editors. He also has experience with desktop graphics applications, game development, large-scale systems for aviation, writing graphics drivers and even biofeedback. In the past, Bartek has also taught programming (mostly game and graphics programming courses) at local universities in Cracow.

Since 2011 Bartek has been regularly blogging at bfilipek.com[18] and lately at cppstories.com[19]. Initially, the topics revolved around graphics programming, but now the blog focuses on core C++. He's also a co-organiser of the C++ User Group in Cracow[20]. You can hear Bartek in one @CppCast episode[21] where he talks about C++17, blogging and text processing.

Since October 2018, Bartek has been a C++ Expert for the Polish National Body which works directly with ISO/IEC JTC 1/SC 22 (C++ Standardisation Committee). In the same month, Bartek was awarded his first MVP title for the years 2019/2020 by Microsoft.

In his spare time, he loves collecting and assembling Lego models with his little son.

Bartek is the author of C++17 In Detail[22].

---

[17]http://www.xara.com/
[18]https://www.bfilipek.com
[19]https://www.cppstories.com]
[20]https://www.meetup.com/C-User-Group-Cracow/
[21]http://cppcast.com/2018/04/bartlomiej-filipek/
[22]https://leanpub.com/cpp17indetail

Acknowledgements

This book wouldn't be possible without valuable input from C++ Expert **Tomasz Kamiński** (see Tomek's profile at Linkedin[23]).

Tomek led a live coding presentation about "history" of lambdas at our local C++ User Group in Cracow:

Lambdas: From C++11 to C++20 - C++ User Group Krakow[24]

A lot of examples used in this book comes from that session.

While the initial version of the book was relatively short, the extended version (additional 100 pages!) was a result of the feedback and encouragement I got from **JFT (John Taylor)**. John spent a lot of time on finding even little things that could be improved and extended.

Also, I'd like to thank **Dawid Pilarski** (panicsoftware.com/about-me[25]) for helpful feedback and a review of the whole book.

Additional words of recognition goes to **Björn Fahller** (@playfulprogramming[26]), **Javier Estrada** (javierestrada.blog[27]) and **Andreas Fertig** (andreasfertig.info[28]) for reviews and extra discussions.

Last but not least, I got a lot of feedback and comments from the blog readers, Patreon Discord Server, and discussions at C++ Polska[29]. Thank you all!

With all of the help from those kind people, the book quality got better and better!

---

[23]https://www.linkedin.com/in/tomasz-kami%C5%84ski-208572b1/
[24]https://www.meetup.com/pl-PL/C-User-Group-Cracow/events/258795519/
[25]https://blog.panicsoftware.com/about-me/
[26]https://playfulprogramming.blogspot.com/
[27]https://javierestrada.blog/
[28]https://andreasfertig.info/
[29]https://cpp-polska.pl/

Revision History

- 25th March 2019 - The First Edition is live!
- 5th January 2020 - Grammar, better examples, wording, IIFE section, C++20 updates,
- 17th April 2020 - The C++20 chapter is rewritten, grammar, wording, layout,
- 30th April 2020 - Deriving from lambdas, in C++11, C++17 and C++20,
- 19th June 2020 - Major update:
  - Improved C++98/03 chapter, added sections about helper functional objects from the Standard Library,
  - Added a new section on how to convert from deprecated `bind1st` into modern alternatives in the C++14 chapter,
  - Improved and extended IFFE section in C++11 and C++17 chapters,
  - New Appendix with a list of lambda techniques,
  - New Appendix with a list of "Top 5 Lambda Features", adapted from a blog article,
  - New title image with updated subtitle,
  - Lots of smaller improvements across the whole book,
- 3rd August 2020 - Major Update, also the Kindle Version available:
  - Most code samples have now a link to an online compiler version in the title,
  - Improved description of the syntax of lambdas, showed differences in C++17 and C++20 chapters,
  - New sections: how to store lambdas in a container, Lambdas and Asynchronous Execution, recursive lambdas, Exception Specification in Type System,
  - New section on variadic generic lambdas in C++14 and C++17,
  - New section on variadic packs in C++11, C++20,
  - Use `const` and `noexcept` in longer examples if possible,
  - Lots of smaller changes, improvements, layout across the whole book.
- 30 November 2020 - Corrections, typos, grammar:
  - Wording for data members, function objects (why not a "functor"),
  - Clarification about capturing, initialisation and generated compiler code,
- 1st February 2021 - Print Version of the book!
  - An extended version of the Appendix "Top 6 Lambda Features",
  - Refactoring with IIFE, diagrams for the lambda syntax, index, layout fixes.

1. Lambdas in C++98/03

To start out, it's good to create some background for our main topic. To do this, we'll move into the past and look at code that doesn't use any modern C++ techniques - which means C++98/03 Specification.

In this chapter, you'll learn:

- How to pass function objects to algorithms from the Standard Library in the "old way".
- The limitations of function object class types.
- Why functional helpers weren't good enough.
- The motivation for lambdas for C++0x/C++11.

Callable Objects in C++98/03

One of the fundamental ideas of the Standard Library is that algorithms like `std::sort`, `std::for_each`, `std::transform` and many others, can take any callable object and call it on elements of the input container. However, in C++98/03, this only included function pointers or class types with the call operator (commonly referred as a "functor").

As an example, let's have a look at an application that prints all elements of a vector.

In the first version we'll use a regular function:

Ex1_1: A basic print function. Live code @Wandbox

```cpp
#include <algorithm>
#include <iostream>
#include <vector>

void PrintFunc(int x) {
    std::cout << x << '\n';
}

int main() {
    std::vector<int> v;
    v.push_back(1); // no uniform initialisation in C++03!
    v.push_back(2); // push_back available only... :)
    std::for_each(v.begin(), v.end(), PrintFunc);
}
```

The code above uses `std::for_each` to iterate over a vector (we use C++98/03 so range-based for loop is not available!) and then it passes `PrintFunc` as a callable object.

We can convert this function into a class type with the call operator:

Ex1_2: A basic print function object type. Live code @Wandbox

```cpp
#include <algorithm>
#include <iostream>
#include <vector>

struct Printer {
    void operator()(int x) const {
        std::cout << x << '\n';
    }
};

int main() {
    std::vector<int> v;
    v.push_back(1);
    v.push_back(2); // no initialiser list in C++98/03...
    std::for_each(v.begin(), v.end(), Printer());
}
```

The Example defines a `struct` with `operator()` so it means that you can "call" this object like a regular function:

```cpp
Printer printer;
printer();              // calls operator()
printer.operator()();   // equivalent call
```

While non-member functions are usually stateless[1], function-like class types can hold non-static data members which allow storing state. One example is to count the number of invocations of a callable object in an algorithm. This solution needs to keep a counter that is updated with each call:

---

[1]You can use globals or static variables in a regular function, but it's not the best solution. Such an approach makes it hard to control the state across many groups of lambda invocations.

Ex1_3: Function object with a state. Live code @Wandbox

```cpp
#include <algorithm>
#include <iostream>
#include <vector>

struct PrinterEx {
    PrinterEx(): numCalls(0) { }

    void operator()(int x) {
        std::cout << x << '\n';
        ++numCalls;
    }

    int numCalls;
};

int main() {
    std::vector<int> v;
    v.push_back(1);
    v.push_back(2);
    const PrinterEx vis = std::for_each(v.begin(), v.end(), PrinterEx());
    std::cout << "num calls: " << vis.numCalls << '\n';
}
```

In the above example, there's a data member numCalls which is used to count the number of invocations of the call operator. std::for_each returns the function object that we passed it, so we can then take this object and get the data member.

As you can easily predict, we should get the following output:

```
1
2
num calls: 2
```

We can also "capture" variables from the calling scope. To do that we have to create a data member in our function object and initialise it in the constructor.

Ex1_4: Function object with a 'captured' variable. Live code @Wandbox

```cpp
#include <algorithm>
#include <iostream>
#include <string>
#include <vector>

struct PrinterEx {
    PrintEx(const std::string& str):
        strText(str), numCalls(0) { }

    void operator()(int x) {
        std::cout << strText << x << '\n';
        ++numCalls;
    }

    std::string strText;
    int numCalls;
};

int main() {
    std::vector<int> v;
    v.push_back(1);
    v.push_back(2);
    const std::string introText("Elem: ");
    const PrinterEx vis = std::for_each(v.begin(), v.end(),
                                        PrinterEx(introText));
    std::cout << "num calls: " << vis.numCalls << '\n';
}
```

In this version, `PrinterEx` takes an extra parameter to initialise a data member. Then this variable is used in the call operator and the expected output is as follows:

```
Elem: 1
Elem: 2
num calls: 2
```

What is a "Functor"?

A few sections above I referred that class types with `operator()` are sometimes called "functors". While this term is handy and much shorter than "function object class type" it's not correct.

As it appears, "Functor" comes from functional programming, and it has a different meaning than colloquially used in C++.

Quoting Bartosz Milewski on Functors[2]:

> A functor is a mapping between categories. Given two categories, C and D, a functor F maps objects in C to objects in D — it's a function on objects.

It's very abstract, but fortunately, we can also look at some simpler definition. In chapter 10 of "Functional Programming in C++"[3] Ivan Cukic "translates" those abstract definitions into more practical one for C++:

> A class template `F` is a functor if it has a `transform` (or `map`) function defined on it.

Also, such a `transform` function must obey two rules about identity and composition.

The term "Functor" is not present in any form in the C++ Specification (even in C++98/03), therefore for the rest of this book, we'll try to avoid it.

I recommend the following sources to read more about Functors:

- Functors, Applicatives, And Monads In Pictures - adit.io[4]
- Functors | Bartosz Milewski's Programming Cafe[5]
- What are C++ functors and their uses? - Stack Overflow[6]
- Functor - Wikipedia[7]

---

[2]https://bartoszmilewski.com/2015/01/20/functors/
[3]"Functional Programming in C++: How to improve your C++ programs using functional techniques 1st Edition" @Amazon
[4]https://adit.io/posts/2013-04-17-functors,_applicatives,_and_monads_in_pictures.html
[5]https://bartoszmilewski.com/2015/01/20/functors/
[6]https://stackoverflow.com/questions/356950/what-are-c-functors-and-their-uses
[7]https://en.wikipedia.org/wiki/Functor

Issues with Function Object Class Types

As you can see, creating class types with the call operator is very powerful. You have full control, and you can design them any way you like.

However, in C++98/03, the problem was that you had to define a function object type in a different place than the invocation of the algorithm. This could mean that the callable could be dozens or hundreds of lines earlier or further in the source file, or even in a different compilation unit.

As a potential solution, you might have tried writing local classes, since C++ always has support for that syntax. But that didn't work with templates.

See this code:

A Local Function Object Type

```
int main() {
    struct LocalPrinter {
        void operator()(int x) const {
            std::cout << x << '\n';
        }
    };

    std::vector<int> v(10, 1);
    std::for_each(v.begin(), v.end(), LocalPrinter());
}
```

Try to compile it with -std=c++98 and you'll see the following error on GCC:

```
error: template argument for
'template<class _IIter, class _Funct> _Funct
std::for_each(_IIter, _IIter, _Funct)'
uses local type 'main()::LocalPrinter'
```

As it appears, in C++98/03, you couldn't instantiate a template with a local type.

C++ programmers quickly understood those limitations and found ways to work around the issues with C++98/03. One solution was to prepare a set of helpers. Let's revise them in the next section.

Composing With Functional Helpers

How about having some helpers and predefined function objects?

If you check the `<functional>` header from the Standard Library, you'll find a lot of types and functions that can be immediately used with the standard algorithms.

For example:

- `std::plus<T>()` - takes two arguments and returns their sum.
- `std::minus<T>()` - takes two arguments and returns their difference.
- `std::less<T>()` - takes two arguments and returns if the first one is smaller than the second.
- `std::greater_equal<T>()` - takes two arguments and returns if the first is greater or equal to the second.
- `std::bind1st` - creates a callable object with the first argument fixed to the given value.
- `std::bind2nd` - creates a callable object with the second argument fixed to the given value.
- `std::mem_fun` - creates a member function wrapper object.
- and many more.

Let's write some code that benefits from the helpers:

Ex1_5: Using old C++98/03 functional helpers. Live code @Wandbox

```
#include <algorithm>
#include <functional>
#include <vector>

int main() {
    std::vector<int> v;
    v.push_back(1);
    v.push_back(2);
    // .. push back until 9...
    const size_t smaller5 = std::count_if(v.begin(), v.end(),
                                std::bind2nd(std::less<int>(), 5));
```

```
    return smaller5;
}
```

The example uses std::less and fixes its second argument by using std::bind2nd. This whole "composition" is passed into count_if[8]. As you can probably guess, the code expands into a function that performs a simple comparison:

```
return x < 5;
```

If you wanted more ready-to-use helpers, then you can also look at the boost library, for example boost::bind.

Unfortunately, the main issue with this approach is the complexity and hard-to-learn syntax. For instance, writing code that composes two or more functions is not natural. Have a look below:

Ex1_6: Composing functional helpers. Live Code @Wandbox

```
#include <algorithm>
#include <functional>
#include <vector>

int main() {
    using std::placeholders::_1;

    std::vector<int> v;
    v.push_back(1);
    v.push_back(2);
    // push_back until 9...
    const size_t val = std::count_if(v.begin(), v.end(),
                             std::bind(std::logical_and<bool>(),
                             std::bind(std::greater<int>(),_1, 2),
                             std::bind(std::less_equal<int>(),_1,6)));

    return val;
}
```

---

[8]bind1st, bind2nd and other functional helpers were deprecated in C++11 and removed in C++17. The code in this chapter uses them only to illustrate C++98/03 issues. Please use some modern alternatives in your projects. See the C++14 chapter for more information.

The composition uses `std::bind` (from C++11, so we cheated a bit, it's not C++98/03) with `std::greater` and `std::less_equal` connected with `std::logical_and`. Additionally, the code uses `_1` which is a placeholder for the first input argument.

While the above code works, and you can define it locally, you probably agree that it's complicated and not natural syntax. Not to mention that this composition represents only a simple condition:

```
return x > 2 && x <= 6;
```

Is there anything better and more straightforward to use?

Motivation for a New Feature

As you can see, in C++98/03, there were several ways to declare and pass a callable object to algorithms and utilities from the Standard Library. However, all of those options were a bit limited. For example, you couldn't declare a local function object types, or it was complicated to compose a function with functional helper objects.

Fortunately with C++11 we finally saw a lot of improvements!

First of all, the C++ Committee lifted the limitation of the template instantiation with a local type. Since C++11 you can write class types with the call operator locally, in the place where you need them.

What's more, C++11 also brought another idea to life: what if we have a short syntax and then the compiler could "expand" it in a local function object type definition?

And that was the birth of "lambda expressions"!

If we look at N3337[9] - the final draft of C++11, we can see a separate section for lambdas: [expr.prim.lambda][10].

Let's have a look at this new feature in the next chapter.

---

[9]https://timsong-cpp.github.io/cppwp/n3337/
[10]https://timsong-cpp.github.io/cppwp/n3337/expr.prim.lambda

2. Lambdas in C++11

Hooray! The C++ Committee listened to the opinions of developers, and since C++11 we got lambda expressions!

Lambdas quickly become one of the most recognisable features of modern C++.

You can read the full specification located under N3337[1] - the final draft of C++11.

And the separate section for lambdas: [expr.prim.lambda][2].

I think the committee added lambdas in a smart way to the language. They incorporate new syntax, but then the compiler "expands" it into an unnamed "hidden" function object type. This way we have all the advantages (and disadvantages) of the real strongly typed language, and it's relatively easy to reason about the code.

In this chapter, you'll learn:

- The basic syntax of lambdas.
- How to capture variables.
- How to capture non-static data members of a class.
- The return type of a lambda.
- What a closure object is.
- How a lambda can be converted to a function pointer and use it with C-style API.
- What's IIFE and why is it useful.
- How to inherit from a lambda expression.

Let's go!

---

[1]https://timsong-cpp.github.io/cppwp/n3337/
[2]https://timsong-cpp.github.io/cppwp/n3337/expr.prim.lambda

The Syntax of Lambda Expression

Below you can find a diagram that illustrates the syntax for lambdas in C++11:

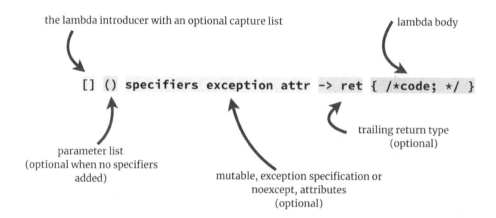

Lambda Syntax in C++11

Let's now see a few examples, just to create some intuition.

A Few Examples of Lambda Expressions

```
// 1. the simplest lambda:
[]{};
```

In the first example, you can see a "minimal" lambda expression. It only needs the [] section (the lambda introducer) and then the empty {} part for the function body. The argument list - () - is optional and not needed in this case.

```
// 2. with two params:
[](float f, int a) { return a * f; };
[](int a, int b) { return a < b; };
```

In the second example, probably one of the most common, you can see that the arguments are passed into the () section, just like for a regular function. The return type is not needed, as the compiler will automatically deduce it.

```
// 3. trailing return type:
[](MyClass t) -> int { auto a = t.compute(); print(a); return a; };
```

In the above example, we explicitly set a return type. The trailing return type is also available for regular function declaration since C++11.

```
// 4. additional specifiers:
[x](int a, int b) mutable { ++x; return a < b; };
[](float param) noexcept { return param*param; };
[x](int a, int b) mutable noexcept { ++x; return a < b; };
```

The last example shows that before the body of the lambda, you can use other specifiers. In the code, we used mutable (so that we can change the captured variable) and also noexcept. The third lambda uses mutable and noexcept and they have to appear in that order (you cannot write noexcept mutable as the compiler rejects it).

While the () part is optional, if you want to apply mutable or noexcept then () needs to be in the expression:

```
// 5. optional ()
[x] { std::cout << x; }; // no () needed
[x] mutable { ++x; };     // won't compile!
[x]() mutable { ++x; };   // fine - () required before mutable
[] noexcept { };          // won't compile!
[]() noexcept { };        // fine
```

The same pattern applies for other specifiers that can be applied on lambdas like constexpr or consteval in C++17 and C++20.

After basic examples, we can now try to understand how it works and learn full possibilities of lambda expressions.

Core Definitions

Before we go further, it's handy to bring some core definitions from the C++ Standard:

From [expr.prim.lambda#2][3]:

> The evaluation of a lambda-expression results in a prvalue temporary. This temporary is called the **closure object**.

As a side note, a lambda expression is a prvalue which is "pure rvalue". This kind of expressions usually yields initialisations and appear on the right-hand side of the assignment (or in a return statement). Read more on C++ Reference[4].

And another definition from [expr.prim.lambda#3][5]:

> The type of the lambda-expression (which is also the type of the closure object) is a unique, unnamed non-union class type — called the **closure type**.

Compiler Expansion

From the above definitions, we can understand that the compiler generates some unique closure type from a lambda expression. Then we can have an instance of this type through the closure object.

Here's a basic example that shows how to write a lambda expression and pass it to `std::for_each`. For comparison, the code also illustrates the corresponding function object type generated by the compiler:

---

[3]https://timsong-cpp.github.io/cppwp/n3337/expr.prim.lambda#2
[4]https://en.cppreference.com/w/cpp/language/value_category
[5]https://timsong-cpp.github.io/cppwp/n3337/expr.prim.lambda#3

Ex2_1: Lambda and a Corresponding Function Object. Live code @WandBox

```cpp
#include <algorithm>
#include <iostream>
#include <vector>

int main() {
    struct {
        void operator()(int x) const {
            std::cout << x << '\n';
        }
    } someInstance;

    const std::vector<int> v { 1, 2, 3 };
    std::for_each(v.cbegin(), v.cend(), someInstance);
    std::for_each(v.cbegin(), v.cend(), [] (int x) {
            std::cout << x << '\n';
        }
    );
}
```

In the example, the compiler transforms...

```cpp
[](int x) { std::cout << x << '\n'; }
```

...into an anonymous function object that in a simplified form can look as follows:

```cpp
struct {
    void operator()(int x) const {
        std::cout << x << '\n';
    }
} someInstance;
```

The process of translation or "expansion" can be easily viewed on C++ Insights[6] an online tool which takes valid C++ code and then produces a source code version that the compiler generates: like anonymous function objects for lambdas, template instantiation and many other C++ features.

In the next sections we'll dive more into the individual parts of the lambda expression.

---

[6]https://cppinsights.io/

The Type of a Lambda Expression

Since the compiler generates a unique name for each lambda (the closure type), there's no way to "spell" it upfront.

That's why you have to use auto (or decltype) to deduce the type.

```cpp
auto myLambda = [](int a) -> double { return 2.0 * a; };
```

What's more, if you have two lambdas that look the same:

```cpp
auto firstLam  = [](int x) { return x * 2; };
auto secondLam = [](int x) { return x * 2; };
```

Their types are different even if the "code-behind" is the same! The compiler is required to declare two unique unnamed types for each lambda.

We can prove this property with the following code:

Ex2_1: Different Types, Same Code. Live code @Wandbox

```cpp
#include <type_traits>

int main() {
    const auto oneLam = [](int x) noexcept { return x * 2; };
    const auto twoLam = [](int x) noexcept { return x * 2; };
    static_assert(!std::is_same<decltype(oneLam), decltype(twoLam)>::value,
                  "must be different!");
}
```

The example above verifies if the closure types for oneLam and twoLam are not the same.

 In C++17 we can use static_assert with no message and also helper variable templates for type traits is_same_v:

```cpp
static_assert(std::is_same_v<double, decltype(baz(10))>);
```

However, while you don't know the exact name, you can spell out the signature of the lambda and then store it in std::function. In general, what can't be done with a lambda defined as auto can be done if the lambda is "expressed" through std::function<> type. For example, the previous lambda has a signature of double(int) as it takes an int as an input parameter and returns double. We can then create a std::function object in the following way:

```
std::function<double(int)> myFunc = [](int a) -> double { return 2.0 * a; };
```

std::function is a heavy object because it needs to handle all callable objects. To do that, it requires advanced internal mechanics like type punning or even dynamic memory allocation. We can check its size in a simple experiment:

Ex2_3: std::function and auto type Deduction. Live code @Wandbox

```
#include <functional>
#include <iostream>

int main() {
    const auto myLambda = [](int a) noexcept -> double {
        return 2.0 * a;
    };

    const std::function<double(int)> myFunc =
        [](int a) noexcept -> double {
            return 2.0 * a;
        };

    std::cout << "sizeof(myLambda) is " << sizeof(myLambda) << '\n';
    std::cout << "sizeof(myFunc) is " << sizeof(myFunc) << '\n';

    return myLambda(10) == myFunc(10);
}
```

On GCC the code will print:

```
sizeof(myLambda) is 1
sizeof(myFunc) is 32
```

Because myLambda is just a stateless lambda, it's also an empty class, without any data member fields, so it's minimal size is only one byte. On the other hand, the std::function version is much larger - 32 bytes. That's why if you can, rely on the `auto` type deduction to get the smallest possible closure objects.

When we talk about `std::function`, it's also important to mention that this type doesn't support moveable-only closures. You can read more about this issue in the C++14 chapter on moveable types.

Constructors and Copying

In the specification of the feature at [expr.prim.lambda][7] we can also read the following:

> The closure type associated with a lambda-expression has a deleted ([dcl.fct.def.delete]) default constructor and a deleted copy assignment operator.

That's why you cannot write:

```
auto foo = [&x, &y]() { ++x; ++y; };
decltype(foo) fooCopy;
```

This gives the following error on GCC:

```
error: use of deleted function 'main()::<lambda()>::<lambda>()'
        decltype(foo) fooCopy;
                      ^~~~~~~
note: a lambda closure type has a deleted default constructor
```

However, you can copy lambdas:

---

[7]https://timsong-cpp.github.io/cppwp/n3337/expr.prim.lambda#19

Ex2_4: Copying lambdas. Live code @Wandbox

```
#include <type_traits>

int main() {
    const auto firstLam = [](int x) noexcept { return x * 2; };
    const auto secondLam = firstLam;
    static_assert(std::is_same<decltype(firstLam), decltype(secondLam)>::value,
                  "must be the same");
}
```

If you copy a lambda, then you also copy its state. This is important when we talk about capture variables. In that context, a closure type stores captured variables as member fields. Performing a lambda copy will copy those data member fields.

A peek into the future

In C++20 a stateless lambda will be default constructible and assignable.

The Call Operator

The code that you put into the lambda body is "translated" to the code in the operator() of the corresponding closure type.

By default, in C++11, it's a const inline member function. For instance:

```
auto lam = [](double param) { /* do something*/ };
```

Expands into something similar as:

```
struct __anonymousLambda {
    inline void operator()(double param) const { /* do something */ }
};
```

Let's discuss the consequences of this approach and how can we modify the resulting call operator declaration.

Overloading

One thing that is worth mentioning is that when you define a lambda there's no way to create "overloaded" lambdas taking different arguments. Like:

```
// doesn't compile!
auto lam = [](double param) { /* do something*/ };
auto lam = [](int param) { /* do something*/ };
```

Above, the code won't compile as the compiler cannot translate those two lambdas in a single function object. Additionally you cannot redefine the same variable. On the other hand, it's possible to create a function object type which has two call operators:

```
struct MyFunctionObject {
    inline void operator()(double param) const { /* do something */ }
    inline void operator()(int param) const { /* do something */ }
};
```

MyFunctionObject can now work with double and int arguments. If you want a similar behaviour for lambdas, then you can see the section about inheriting from lambdas in this chapter and also about the overloaded pattern from the C++17 chapter.

Attributes

The syntax for lambdas allows using C++11's attributes in the form of [[attr_name]]. However, if you apply an attribute to a lambda, then it applies to the type of the call operator and not to the operator itself. That's why currently (and even in C++20) there are no attributes that make sense to put on a lambda. Most compilers even report an error. If we take a C++17 attribute and try to use it with the expression:

```
auto myLambda = [](int a) [[nodiscard]] { return a * a; };
```

This generates the following error on Clang (see live code @Wandbox[8]):

---

[8]https://wandbox.org/permlink/3zfzL1NNpPXXgLOx

```
error: 'nodiscard' attribute cannot be applied to types
```

While in theory the lambda syntax is prepared, at the moment there are no applicable attributes.

Other Modifiers

We briefly touched on this topic in the syntax section, but you're not limited to a default declaration of the call operator for a closure type. In C++11 you can add `mutable` or an exception specification.

 If possible longer examples of this book try to mark the closure object with `const` and also make the lambda `noexcept`.

You can use those keywords by specifying `mutable` and `noexcept` after the parameter declaration clause:

```
auto myLambda = [](int a) mutable noexcept { /* do something */ }
```

The compiler will expand this code into:

```
struct __anonymousLambda {
    inline void operator()(double param) noexcept { /* do something */ }
};
```

Please notice that the `const` keyword is gone now and the call operator can now change the data members of the lambda.

But what data members? How can we declare a data member of lambdas? See the next section about "capturing" variables:

Captures

The `[]` does not only introduce the lambda but also holds a list of captured variables. It's called *"capture clause"*.

By capturing a variable from the outside scope of the lambda, you create a non-static data member in the closure type. Then, inside the lambda body, you can access it.

We did a similar thing for the `Printer` function object in the C++98/03 chapter. In that class, we added a data member `std::string strText` which was initialised in the constructor. Having a data member allows us to store state in the callable object.

The syntax for captures in C++11:

Syntax	Description
[&]	capture by reference all automatic storage duration variables declared in the reaching scope
[=]	capture by value (create a copy) all automatic storage duration variables declared in the reaching scope
[x, &y]	capture x by value and y by a reference explicitly
[args...]	capture a template argument pack, all by value
[&args...]	capture a template argument pack, all by reference
[this]	captures the this pointer inside the member function

Please note that for [=] and [&] cases, the compiler generates data members for all used variables inside the lambda body. This is a convenient syntax where you don't want to explicitly mention which variables you capture.

Here's a summary of the basic syntax with examples:

```
int x = 2, y = 3;

const auto l1 = []()  { return 1; };          // No capture
const auto l2 = [=]() { return x; };          // All variables used in
                                              // the lambda are copied
const auto l3 = [&]() { return y; };          // All variables used in
                                              // the lambda are referenced
const auto l4 = [x]() { return x; };          // Only x by value (copy)
// const auto lx = [=x]() { return x; };      // wrong syntax, no need for
                                              // = to copy x explicitly
const auto l5 = [&y]()   { return y; };       // Only y by ref
const auto l6 = [x, &y]() { return x * y; };  // x by value and y by ref
const auto l7 = [=, &x]() { return x + y; };  // All by value except x
                                              // which is by ref
const auto l8 = [&, y]() { return x - y; };   // All by ref except y which
                                              // is by value
```

What is "Automatic Storage Duration" ?

All objects in a program have four possible ways to be "stored": automatic, static, thread or dynamic. Automatic means that the storage is allocated at the start of a scope, like in a function. Most local variables have automatic storage duration (except for those declared as static, extern or thread_local). See more @CppReference - storage duration[9].

To understand what happens with a captured variable let's consider the following code:

```
std::string str {"Hello World"};
auto foo = [str]() { std::cout << str << '\n'; };
foo();
```

For the above lambda, str is captured by value (i.e. it is copied). The compiler might generate the following local function object:

```
struct _unnamedLambda {
    inline void operator()() const {
        std::cout << str << '\n';
    }

    std::string str;
};
```

When you pass a variable into the capture clause it is then used to direct initialise the data member str. So the previous example can "expand" into:

```
std::string str {"Hello World"};
_unnamedLambda foo { str };
foo();
```

To be precise the standard mentions this behaviour in [expr.prim.lambda#21][10]:

---

[9]https://en.cppreference.com/w/cpp/language/storage_duration
[10]https://timsong-cpp.github.io/cppwp/n3337/expr.prim.lambda#21

> When the lambda-expression is evaluated, the entities that are captured by copy are used to direct-initialise each corresponding non-static data member of the resulting closure object.

And another example with two variables:

```
int x = 1, y = 1;
std::cout << x << " " << y << '\n';
const auto foo = [&x, &y]() noexcept { ++x; ++y; };
foo();
std::cout << x << " " << y << '\n';
```

For the above lambda, the compiler might generate the following local function object:

```
struct _unnamedLambda {
    void operator()() const noexcept {
        ++x; ++y;
    }

    int& x;
    int& y;
};
```

Since we capture x and y by reference, the closure type will contain two data members which are also references.

 The value of the value-captured variable is at the time the lambda is defined - not when it is used! The value of a ref-captured variable is the value when the lambda is used - not when it is defined.

 The C++ closures do not extend the lifetimes of the captured references. Be sure that the capture variable still lives when lambda is invoked.

Generated Code

Across this book, I show a possible compiler-generated code as a `struct` to define a closure class type. However, this is only a simplification - a mental model - and inside the compiler, it might be different.

For example, in Clang, the generated AST (Abstract Syntax Tree) uses `class` to represent a closure. The call operator is defined as `public` while data members are `private`.

That's why you cannot write:

```
int x = 0;
auto lam = [x]() { std::cout << x; };
lam.x = 10; // ??
```

In GCC (or similarly in Clang) you'll get:

```
error: 'struct main()::<lambda()>' has no member named 'x'
```

On the other hand, we have an essential part of the specification which mentions, that captured variables are direct initialised, which is impossible for private members (for our regular classes in code). This means that compilers can do a bit "magic" here and create more efficient code (there's no need to copy variables or even move them).

You can read more about the Lambdas internals in a great blog post by Andreas Fertig (the creator of C++ Insights): Under the covers of C++ lambdas - Part 2: Captures, captures, captures[11].

Capture All or Explicit?

While specifying `[=]` or `[&]` might be convenient, as it captures all automatic storage duration variables, it's clearer to capture a variable explicitly. That way the compiler can warn you about unwanted effects (see notes about global and static variable for example).

You can also read more in item 31 in "Effective Modern C++"[12] by Scott Meyers: "Avoid default capture modes."

---

[11]https://andreasfertig.blog/2020/11/under-the-covers-of-cpp-lambdas-part-2-captures-captures-captures/
[12]"Effective Modern C++: 42 Specific Ways to Improve Your Use of C++11 and C++14" 1st Edition by Scott Meyers, 2014

The `mutable` Keyword

By default the `operator()` of the closure type is marked as `const`, and you cannot modify captured variables inside the body of the lambda.

If you want to change this behaviour, you need to add the `mutable` keyword after the parameter list. This syntax effectively removes the `const` from the call operator declaration in the closure type. If you have a simple lambda expression with a `mutable`:

```
int x = 1;
auto foo = [x]() mutable { ++x; };
```

It will be "expanded" into the following function object:

```
struct __lambda_x1 {
    void operator()() { ++x; }
    int x;
};
```

As you can see, the call operator can change the value of the member fields.

Ex2_5: Capturing Two Variables by Copy and Mutable. Live code @Wandbox

```
#include <iostream>

int main() {
    const auto print = [](const char* str, int x, int y) {
        std::cout << str << ": " << x << " " << y << '\n';
    };
    int x = 1, y = 1;
    print("in main()", x, y);
    auto foo = [x, y, &print]() mutable {
        ++x;
        ++y;
        print("in foo()", x, y);
    };
    foo();
    print("in main()", x, y);
}
```

Output:

```
in main(): 1 1
in foo(): 2 2
in main(): 1 1
```

In the above example, we can change the values of x and y. Since those are only the copies of x and y from the enclosing scope, we don't see their new values after foo is invoked.

On the other hand, if you capture by reference you don't need to apply mutable to the lambda to modify the value. This is because the captured data members are references which means you cannot rebound them to a new object anyway, but you can change the referenced values.

```
int x = 1;
std::cout << x << '\n';
const auto foo = [&x]() noexcept { ++x; };
foo();
std::cout << x << '\n';
```

In the above example, the lambda is not specified with mutable but it can change the referenced value.

One important thing to notice is that when you apply mutable, then you cannot mark your resulting closure object with const as it prevents you from invoking the lambda!

```
int x = 10;
const auto lam = [x]() mutable { ++x; }
lam(); // doesn't compile!
```

The last line won't compile as we cannot call a non-const member function on a const object.

Invocation Counter - An Example of Captured Variables

Before we move on to some more complicated topics with capturing, we can have a little break and focus on a more practical example.

Lambda expressions are handy when you want to use some existing algorithm from the Standard Library and alter the default behaviour. For example, for std::sort you can write your comparison function.

But we can go further and enhance the comparator with an invocation counter. Have a look:

Ex2_6: Invocation Counter. Live code @Compiler Explorer

```cpp
#include <algorithm>
#include <iostream>
#include <vector>

int main() {
    std::vector<int> vec { 0, 5, 2, 9, 7, 6, 1, 3, 4, 8 };

    size_t compCounter = 0;
    std::sort(vec.begin(), vec.end(),
        [&compCounter](int a, int b) noexcept {
            ++compCounter;
            return a < b;
        }
    );

    std::cout << "number of comparisons: " << compCounter << '\n';

    for (const auto& v : vec)
        std::cout << v << ", ";
}
```

The comparator provided in the example works in the same way as the default one, it returns if a is smaller than b, so we use the natural order from lowest to the largest numbers. However, the lambda passed to `std::sort` also captures a local variable `compCounter`. The variable is then used to count all of the invocations of this comparator from the sorting algorithm.

Capturing Global Variables

If you have a global variable and you use `[=]` in your lambda, you might think that your global object is also captured by value... but it's not. See the code:

Ex2_7: Capturing Globals. Live code @Wandbox

```cpp
#include <iostream>

int global = 10;

int main() {
    std::cout << global << '\n';
    auto foo = [=]() mutable noexcept { ++global; };
    foo();
    std::cout << global << '\n';
    const auto increaseGlobal = []() noexcept { ++global; };
    increaseGlobal();
    std::cout << global << '\n';
    const auto moreIncreaseGlobal = [global]() noexcept { ++global; };
    moreIncreaseGlobal();
    std::cout << global << '\n';
}
```

The above example defines `global` and then uses it with several lambdas defined in the `main()` function. If you run the code, then no matter the way you capture, it will always point to the global object, and no local copies will be created.

It's because only variables with automatic storage duration can be captured. GCC can even report the following warning:

```
warning: capture of variable 'global' with non-automatic
         storage duration
```

This warning will appear only if you explicitly capture a global variable, so if you use `[=]` the compiler won't help you.

The Clang compiler is even more helpful, as it generates **an error**:

```
error: 'global' cannot be captured because it does not have
       automatic storage duration
```

See Clang live example @Wandbox[13].

---

[13]https://wandbox.org/permlink/4V91bkuz8NvHrDDA

Capturing Statics

Similarly to capturing global variables, you'll get the same issues with static objects:

Ex2_8: Capturing Static Variables. Live code @Wandbox

```cpp
#include <iostream>

void bar() {
    static int static_int = 10;
    std::cout << static_int << '\n';
    auto foo = [=]() mutable noexcept{ ++static_int; };
    foo();
    std::cout << static_int << '\n';
    const auto increase = []() noexcept { ++static_int; };
    increase();
    std::cout << static_int << '\n';
    const auto moreIncrease = [static_int]() noexcept { ++static_int; };
    moreIncrease();
    std::cout << static_int << '\n';
}

int main() {
    bar();
}
```

This time we try to capture a static variable and then change its value, but since it has no automatic storage duration, the compiler cannot do it.

The output:

```
10
11
12
13
```

GCC reports a warning when you capture the variable by name [static_int] and Clang shows an error.

Capturing a Class Member And the `this` Pointer

Things get a bit more complicated where you're in a class member function, and you want to capture a data member. Since all non-static data members are related to the `this` pointer, it also has to be stored somewhere.

Have a look:

Ex2_9: Error when capturing a data member. Live code @Wandbox

```
#include <iostream>

struct Baz {
    void foo() {
        const auto lam = [s]() { std::cout << s; };
        lam();
    }

    std::string s;
};

int main() {
    Baz b;
    b.foo();
}
```

The code tries to capture s which is a data member. But the compiler will emit the following error message:

```
In member function 'void Baz::foo()':
error: capture of non-variable 'Baz::s'
error: 'this' was not captured for this lambda function
```

To solve this issue, you have to capture the `this` pointer. Then you'll have access to data members.

We can update the code to:

```
struct Baz {
    void foo() {
        const auto lam = [this]() { std::cout << s; };
        lam();
    }

    std::string s;
};
```

There are no compiler errors now.

You can also use [=] or [&] to capture this (they both have the same effect in C++11/14!).

Please notice that we captured this by value... to a pointer. That's why you have access to the initial data member, not its copy.

In C++11 (and even in C++14) you cannot write:

```
auto lam = [*this]() { std::cout << s; };
```

The code won't compile in C++11/14; it is, however, allowed in C++17.

If you use your lambdas in the context of a single method, then capturing this will be fine. But how about more complicated cases?

Do you know what will happen with the following code?

Ex2_10: Returning a Lambda From a Method

```
#include <functional>
#include <iostream>

struct Baz {
    std::function<void()> foo() {
        return [=] { std::cout << s << '\n'; };
    }

    std::string s;
};

int main() {
    auto f1 = Baz{"abc"}.foo();
```

```
    auto f2 = Baz{"xyz"}.foo();
    f1();
    f2();
}
```

The code declares a `Baz` object and then invokes `foo()`. Please note that `foo()` returns a lambda (stored in `std::function`) that captures a member of the class[14].

Since we use temporary objects, we cannot be sure what will happen when you call `f1` and `f2`. This is a dangling reference problem and generates Undefined Behaviour.

Similarly to:

```
struct Bar {
    std::string const& foo() const { return s; };
    std::string s;
};
auto&& f1 = Bar{"abc"}.foo(); // a dangling reference
```

Play with code @Wandbox[15].

If you state the capture explicitly (`[s]`) you'll get a compiler error.

```
std::function<void()> foo() {
    return [s] { std::cout << s << '\n'; };
} // error: 'this' was not captured!
```

All in all, capturing `this` might get tricky when a lambda can outlive the object itself. This might happen when you use async calls or multithreading.

We'll return to that topic in the C++17 chapter. See the "Concurrent Execution Using Lambdas" in the C++17 chapter on page 99.

Moveable-only Objects

If you have an object that is moveable only (for example a `unique_ptr`), then you cannot move it to a lambda as a captured variable. Capturing by value does not work; you can only capture by reference.

---

[14]`std::function` is required in C++11 as there's no return type deduction for functions. This limitation is lifted in C++14.
[15]https://wandbox.org/permlink/FOgbNGoQHOmepBgY

```
std::unique_ptr<int> p(new int{10});
auto foo = [p]() {};        // does not compile....
auto foo_ref = [&p]() { }; // compiles, but the ownership
                            // is not passed
```

In the above example, you can see that the only way to capture `unique_ptr` is by reference. This approach, however, might not be the best as it doesn't transfer the ownership of the pointer.

In the next chapter about C++14, you'll see that this issue is fixed thanks to the capture with initialiser. Go to "Move" section in the C++14 chapter (page 57) to follow up on this topic.

Preserving Const

If you capture a `const` variable, then the constness is preserved:

Ex2_11: Preserving **const**. Live code @Wandbox

```
#include <iostream>
#include <type_traits>

int main() {
    const int x = 10;
    auto foo = [x] () mutable {
        std::cout << std::is_const<decltype(x)>::value << '\n';
        x = 11;
    };
    foo();
}
```

The above code doesn't compile as the captured variable is constant. Here's a possible generated function object for this example:

```
struct __lambda_x {
    void operator()() { x = 11; /*error!*/ }
    const int x;
};
```

You can also play with this code @CppInsight[16].

Capturing a Parameter Pack

To close off our discussion on the capture clause, we should mention that you can also leverage captures with variadic templates. The compiler expands the pack into a list of non-static data members which might be handy if you want to use lambda in a templated code. For example, here's a code sample that experiments with the captures:

Ex2_12: Capturing a Variadic Pack. Live code @Wandbox

```cpp
#include <iostream>
#include <tuple>

template<class... Args>
void captureTest(Args... args) {
    const auto lambda = [args...] {
        const auto tup = std::make_tuple(args...);
        std::cout << "tuple size: " <<
                    std::tuple_size<decltype(tup)>::value << '\n';
        std::cout << "tuple 1st:  " << std::get<0>(tup) << '\n';
    };
    lambda(); // call it
}

int main() {
    captureTest(1, 2, 3, 4);
    captureTest("Hello world", 10.0f);
}
```

After running the code, we'll get the following output:

```
tuple size: 4
tuple 1st:  1
tuple size: 2
tuple 1st:  Hello world
```

This somewhat experimental code shows that you can capture a variadic parameter pack by value (by reference is also possible) and then the pack is "stored" into a tuple object. We then call some helper functions on the tuple to access its data and properties.

You can also use C++Insights to see how the compiler generates the code and expands templates, parameter packs and lambdas into code. See the example here @C++Insight[17].

 See the C++14 chapter where it's possible to capture moveable only type and also in the C++20 chapter for improvements on variadic parameter pack.

Return Type

In most cases, even in C++11, you can skip the return type of the lambda and then the compiler will deduce the typename for you.

As a side note: Initially, return type deduction was restricted to lambdas with bodies containing a single return statement. However, this restriction was quickly lifted as there were no issues with implementing a more convenient version.

See C++ Standard Core Language Defect Reports and Accepted Issues[18].

To sum up, since C++11, the compiler has been able to deduce the return type as long as all of your return statements are of the same type.

From the defect report we can read the following[19]:

..If a *lambda-expression* does not include a *trailing-return-type*, it is as if the *trailing-return-type* denotes the following type:

- if there are no return statements in the compound-statement, or all return statements return either an expression of type void or no expression or braced-init-list, the type void;
- otherwise, if all return statements return an expression and the types of the returned expressions after lvalue-to-rvalue conversion (7.3.2 [conv.lval]), array-to-pointer conversion (7.3.3 [conv.array]), and function-to-pointer conversion (7.3.4 [conv.func]) are the same, that common type;
- otherwise, the program is ill-formed.

---

[17]https://cppinsights.io/s/19d3a45d
[18]http://www.open-std.org/jtc1/sc22/wg21/docs/cwg_defects.html#975
[19]Thanks to Tomek Kamiński for finding the correct link!

Ex2_13: Return Type Deduction. Live code @Wandbox

```
#include <type_traits>

int main() {
    const auto baz = [](int x) noexcept {
        if (x < 20)
            return x * 1.1;
        else
            return x * 2.1;
    };
    static_assert(std::is_same<double, decltype(baz(10))>::value,
                  "has to be the same!");
}
```

In the above lambda, we have two return statements, but they all point to double so the compiler can deduce the type.

 In C++14 the return type of a lambda will be updated to adapt to the rules of auto type deduction for regular functions. See "Return Type Deduction" on page 52. This results in a much simpler definition.

Trailing Return Type Syntax

If you want to be explicit about the return type, you can use trailing return type specification. For example, when you return a string literal:

Ex2_14: Returning a string literal from a lambda

```
#include <iostream>
#include <string>

int main() {
    const auto testSpeedString = [](int speed) noexcept {
        if (speed > 100)
            return "you're a super fast";

        return "you're a regular";
```

```
    };

    auto str = testSpeedString(100);
    str += " driver";                              // oops! no += on const char*!

    std::cout << str;

    return 0;
}
```

The above code doesn't compile because the compiler deduces `const char*` as the return type for the lambda. It's because there's no += operator available on string literals, so the code breaks.

We can fix the problem by explicitly setting the return type to `std::string`:

```
auto testSpeedString = [](int speed) -> std::string {
    if (speed > 100)
        return "you're a super fast";

    return "you're a regular";
};

auto str = testSpeedString(100);
str += " driver"; // works fine
```

You can play with the code @Coliru[20].

Please notice that we had to remove `noexcept` now, as the `std::string` creation might throw.

As a side note, you can also use namespace `std::string_literals;` and then you return `"you're a regular"`s to indicate the `std::string` type.

---

[20]http://coliru.stacked-crooked.com/a/45cebc8b35d5b2a9

Conversion to a Function Pointer

If your lambda doesn't capture any variables then the compiler can convert it to a regular function pointer. See the following description from the Standard expr.prim.lambda#6[21]:

> The closure type for a lambda-expression with no lambda-capture has a public non-virtual non-explicit const conversion function to pointer to function having the same parameter and return types as the closure type's function call operator. The value returned by this conversion function shall be the address of a function that, when invoked, has the same effect as invoking the closure type's function call operator.

To illustrate how a lambda can support such conversion let's consider the following example. It defines a function object baz that explicitly defines the conversion operator:

Ex2_15: Conversion to a Function Pointer. **Live code @Wandbox** line-numbers=on

```cpp
#include <iostream>

void callWith10(void(* bar)(int)) { bar(10); }

int main() {
    struct {
        using f_ptr = void(*)(int);

        void operator()(int s) const { return call(s); }
        operator f_ptr() const { return &call; }

    private:
        static void call(int s) { std::cout << s << '\n'; };
    } baz;

    callWith10(baz);
    callWith10([](int x) { std::cout << x << '\n'; });
}
```

---

[21]https://timsong-cpp.github.io/cppwp/n3337/expr.prim.lambda#6

In the preceding program, there's a function `callWith10` that takes a function pointer. Then we call it with two arguments (lines 18 and 19): the first one uses `baz` which is a function object type that contains necessary conversion operator - it converts to `f_ptr` which is the same as the input parameter for `callWith10`. Later, we have a call with a lambda. In this case, the compiler performs the required conversions underneath.

Such conversion might be handy when you need to call a C-style function that requires some callback. For example, below you can find code that calls `qsort` from the C Library and uses a lambda to sort elements in the reverse order:

Ex2_16: Calling a C-style function. Live code @Wandbox

```cpp
#include <cstdlib>
#include <iostream>

int main () {
    int values[] = { 8, 9, 2, 5, 1, 4, 7, 3, 6 };
    constexpr size_t numElements = sizeof(values)/sizeof(values[0]);

    std::qsort(values, numElements, sizeof(int),
        [](const void* a, const void* b) noexcept {
            return ( *(int*)b - *(int*)a );
        }
    );

    for (const auto& val : values)
        std::cout << val << ", ";
}
```

As you can see in the code sample uses `std::qsort` which takes only function pointers as the comparator. The compiler can do an implicit conversion of the stateless lambda that we pass.

A Tricky Case

Before we move on to another topic there's also one case that might be interesting to analyse:

Ex2_17: Plus and a Lambda. Live code @Wandbox

```cpp
#include <type_traits>

int main() {
        auto funcPtr = +[]{};
        static_assert(std::is_same<decltype(funcPtr), void (*)()>::value);
}
```

Please notice the strange syntax with +. If you remove the plus sign then the `static_assert` fails. Why is that?

To understand how it works we can look at the output generated by the C++ Insights project. See the working example[22]:

```cpp
using FuncPtr_4 = void (*)();
FuncPtr_4 funcPtr =
    +static_cast<void (*)()>(__la.operator __la::retType_4_18());
/* PASSED: static_assert(std::integral_constant<bool, 1>::value); */

// __la is __lambda_4_18 in cppinsights
```

The code uses + which is a unary operator. This operator can work on pointers, so the compiler converts our stateless lambda into a function pointer and then assigns it to `funcPtr`. On the other hand, if you remove the plus, then `funcPtr` is just a regular closure object, and that's why the `static_assert` fails.

While it's probably not the best idea to write such a syntax with "+", it has the same effect if you write `static_cast`. You can apply this technique in a situation when you don't want the compiler to create too many function instantiations. For example:

---

[22]https://cppinsights.io/s/0ee4cd81

Ex2_18: Casting to a Function Pointer. Live code @Cpp Insights

```cpp
template<typename F>
void call_function(F f) {
  f(10);
}

int main() {
    call_function(static_cast<int (*)(int)>([](int x){
        return x + 2; }));
    call_function(static_cast<int (*)(int)>([](int x){
        return x * 2; }));
}
```

In the above example, the compiler has to create only a single instantiation of `call_-function` - as it only takes a function pointer `int (*)(int)`. But if you remove `static_-casts` then you'll get two versions of `call_function` as the compiler has to create two separate types for lambdas.

IIFE - Immediately Invoked Functional Expression

In most of examples you've seen so far, you can notice that I defined a lambda and then called it later.

However, you can also invoke a lambda immediately:

Ex2_19: Calling Lambda Immediately. Live code @Wandbox

```cpp
#include <iostream>

int main() {
    int x = 1, y = 1;
    [&]() noexcept { ++x; ++y; }(); // <-- call ()
    std::cout << x << ", " << y;
}
```

As you can see above, the lambda is created and isn't assigned to any closure object. But then it's called with `()`. If you run the program, you can expect to see `2, 2` as the output.

This kind of expression might be useful when you have a complex initialisation of a `const` object.

```
const auto val = []() {
    /* several lines of code... */
}(); // call it!
```

Above, `val` is a constant value of a type returned by a lambda expression, i.e.:

```
// val1 is int
const auto val1 = []() { return 10; }();

// val2 is std::string
const auto val2 = []() -> std::string { return "ABC"; }();
```

Below you can find a longer example where we use IIFE as a helper lambda to create a constant value inside a function:

Ex2_20: IIFE and HTML Generation. Live code @Wandbox

```
#include <iostream>
#include <string>

void ValidateHTML(const std::string&) { }

std::string BuildAHref(const std::string& link, const std::string& text) {
    const std::string html = [&link, &text] {
        const auto& inText = text.empty() ? link : text;
        return "<a href=\"" + link + "\">" + inText + "</a>";
    }(); // call!

    ValidateHTML(html);

    return html;
}

int main() {
    try {
        const auto ahref = BuildAHref("www.leanpub.com", "Leanpub Store");
        std::cout << ahref;
    }
    catch (...) {
```

```
        std::cout << "bad format...";
    }
}
```

The above example contains a function BuildAHref which takes two parameters and then builds a <a> </a> HTML tag. Based on the input parameters, we build the html variable. If the text is not empty, then we use it as the internal HTML value. Otherwise, we use the link. We want the html variable to be const, yet it's hard to write compact code with the required conditions on the input arguments. Thanks to IIFE we can write a separate lambda and then mark our variable with const. Later the variable can be passed to ValidateHTML.

One Note About the Readability

Sometimes having a lambda which is immediately invoked might cause some readability issues.

For example:

```
const auto EnableErrorReporting = [&]() {
    if (HighLevelWarningEnabled())
        return true;

    if (MidLevelWarningEnabled())
        return UsersWantReporting(); // depends on user settings...

    return false;
}();

if (EnableErrorReporting) {
    // ...
}
```

In the above example, the lambda code is quite complicated, and developers who read the code have to decipher not only that the lambda is invoked immediately, but also they will have to reason about the EnableErrorReporting type. They might assume that EnableErrorReporting is the closure object and not just a const variable. For such cases, you might consider not using auto so that we can easily see the type. And maybe even add a comment next to the }(), like // call it now.

More on IIFE:

You may want to read the chapter about C++17 changes and see an upgraded version of IIFE, starting from page 87.

Inheriting from a Lambda

It might be surprising to see, but you can also derive from a lambda!

Since the compiler expands a lambda expression into a function object with `operator()`, then we can inherit from this type.

Have a look at the basic code:

Ex2_21: Inheriting from a single Lambda. Live code @Wandbox

```cpp
#include <iostream>

template<typename Callable>
class ComplexFn : public Callable {
public:
    explicit ComplexFn(Callable f) : Callable(f) {}
};

template<typename Callable>
ComplexFn<Callable> MakeComplexFunctionObject(Callable&& cal) {
    return ComplexFn<Callable>(std::forward<Callable>(cal));
}

int main() {
    const auto func = MakeComplexFunctionObject([]() {
        std::cout << "Hello Complex Function Object!";
    });
    func();
}
```

In the example, there's the `ComplexFn` class which derives from `Callable` which is a template parameter. If we want to derive from a lambda, we need to do a little trick, as we cannot spell out the exact type of the closure type (unless we wrap it into a `std::function`). That's why we need the `MakeComplexFunctionObject` function that can perform the template argument deduction and get the type of the lambda closure.

The `ComplexFn`, apart from its name, is just a simple wrapper without much of a use. Are there any use cases for such code patterns?

For example, we can extend the code above and inherit from two lambdas and create an overloaded set:

Ex2_22: Inheriting from two Lambdas. Live code @Wandbox

```cpp
#include <iostream>

template<typename TCall, typename UCall>
class SimpleOverloaded : public TCall, UCall {
public:
    SimpleOverloaded(TCall tf, UCall uf) : TCall(tf), UCall(uf) {}

    using TCall::operator();
    using UCall::operator();
};

template<typename TCall, typename UCall>
SimpleOverloaded<TCall, UCall> MakeOverloaded(TCall&& tf, UCall&& uf) {
    return SimpleOverloaded<TCall, UCall>(std::forward<TCall> tf,
                                          std::forward<UCall> uf);
}

int main() {
    const auto func = MakeOverloaded(
        [](int) { std::cout << "Int!\n"; },
        [](float) { std::cout << "Float!\n"; }
    );
    func(10);
    func(10.0f);
}
```

This time we have a bit more code: we derive from two template parameters, but we also need to expose their call operators explicitly.

Why is that? It's because when looking for the correct function overload the compiler requires the candidates to be in the same scope.

To understand that, let's write a simple type that derives from two base classes. The example also comments out two using statements:

Ex2_23: Deriving from two classes, error. Live code @Wandbox

```cpp
#include <iostream>

struct BaseInt {
    void Func(int) { std::cout << "BaseInt...\n"; }
};

struct BaseDouble {
    void Func(double) { std::cout << "BaseDouble...\n"; }
};

struct Derived : public BaseInt, BaseDouble {
    //using BaseInt::Func;
    //using BaseDouble::Func;
};

int main() {
    Derived d;
    d.Func(10.0);
}
```

We have two base classes which implement Func. We want to call that method from the derived object.

GCC reports the following error:

```
error: request for member 'Func' is ambiguous
```

Because we commented out the using statements ::Func() can be from a scope of BaseInt or BaseDouble. The compiler has two scopes to search the best candidate, and according to the Standard, it's not allowed.

Ok, let's go back to our primary use case:

SimpleOverloaded is an elementary class, and it's not production-ready. Have a look at the C++17 chapter where we'll discuss an advanced version of this pattern. Thanks to several C++17 features, we'll be able to inherit from multiple lambdas (thanks to variadic templates) and leverage more compact syntax!

Storing Lambdas in a Container

As the final technique in this chapter, let's have a look at the problem of storing closures in a container.

But didn't I write that lambdas could not be default created and assigned?

Yes... however, we can do some tricks here.

One of the techniques is to leverage the property of stateless lambdas which convert to function pointers. While you cannot store closure objects directly, you can save function pointers converted from lambda expressions.

For example:

Ex2_24: Storing Lambdas As Function Pointers. Live code @Wandbox

```cpp
#include <iostream>
#include <vector>

int main() {
    using TFunc = void (*)(int&);
    std::vector<TFunc> ptrFuncVec;

    ptrFuncVec.push_back([](int& x) { std::cout << x << '\n'; });
    ptrFuncVec.push_back([](int& x) { x *= 2; });
    ptrFuncVec.push_back(ptrFuncVec[0]); // print it again;

    int x = 10;
    for (const auto &entry : ptrFuncVec)
        entry(x);
}
```

In the above example, we create a `vector` of function pointers that will be applied to the variable. There are three entries in the container:

- The first one prints the value of the input argument.
- The second one modifies the value.
- The third is a copy of the first, so it also prints the value.

The solution works, but it's limited to stateless lambdas only. What if we wanted to lift this restriction?

To solve this issue we can reach for the heavy helper: std::function. To make the example interesting, it also switched from simple integers to lambdas that process std::string objects:

Ex2_25: Storing Lambdas As std::function. Live code @Wandbox

```cpp
#include <algorithm>
#include <functional>
#include <iostream>
#include <vector>

int main() {
    std::vector<std::function<std::string(const std::string&)>> vecFilters;

    size_t removedSpaceCounter = 0;
    const auto removeSpaces = [&removedSpaceCounter](const std::string& str) {
        std::string tmp;
        std::copy_if(str.begin(), str.end(), std::back_inserter(tmp),
                    [](char ch) {return !isspace(ch); });
        removedSpaceCounter += str.length() - tmp.length();
        return tmp;
    };

    const auto makeUpperCase = [](const std::string& str) {
        std::string tmp = str;
        std::transform(tmp.begin(), tmp.end(), tmp.begin(),
                [](unsigned char c){ return std::toupper(c); });
        return tmp;
    };

    vecFilters.emplace_back(removeSpaces);
    vecFilters.emplace_back([](const std::string& x) {
                        return x + " Amazing"; });
    vecFilters.emplace_back([](const std::string& x) {
                        return x + " Modern"; });
    vecFilters.emplace_back([](const std::string& x) {
                        return x + " C++"; });
    vecFilters.emplace_back([](const std::string& x) {
```

```
                              return x + " World!"; });
    vecFilters.emplace_back(makeUpperCase);

    const std::string str = "   H e l l o    ";
    auto temp = str;
    for (const auto &entryFunc : vecFilters)
        temp = entryFunc(temp);
    std::cout << temp;

    std::cout <<"\nremoved spaces: " << removedSpaceCounter << '\n';
}
```

The output:

```
HELLO AMAZING MODERN C++ WORLD!
removed spaces: 12
```

This time we store `std::function<std::string(const std::string&)>` in the container. This allows us to use any kind of functional objects, including lambda expressions with captured variables. One of the lambdas `removeSpacesCnt` captures a variable which is used to store the information about the removed spaces from an input string.

Summary

In this chapter, you learned how to create and use lambda expressions. I described the syntax, capture clause, type of the lambda, and we covered lots of examples and use cases. We even went a bit further, and I showed you a pattern of deriving from a lambda or storing it in a container.

But that's not all!

Lambda expressions have become a significant part of Modern C++. With more use cases developers also saw possibilities to improve this feature. And that's why you can now move to the next chapter and see essential updates that the ISO Committee added in C++14.

3. Lambdas in C++14

C++14 added two significant enhancements to lambda expressions:

- Captures with an initialiser
- Generic lambdas

Plus, the Standard also updated some rules, for example:

- Default parameters for lambdas
- Return type as `auto`

These features can solve several issues that were visible in C++11.

You can see the specification in N4140[1] and lambdas: [expr.prim.lambda][2].

What's more, in this chapter, you'll learn about:

- Capturing non-static data members
- Replacing old functional stuff like `std::bind1st` with modern techniques
- LIFTING
- Recursive Lambdas

---

[1]https://timsong-cpp.github.io/cppwp/n4140/
[2]https://timsong-cpp.github.io/cppwp/n4140/expr.prim.lambda

Default Parameters for Lambdas

Let's start with some smaller updates:

In C++14 you can use default parameters in a function call. This is a small feature but makes a lambda more like a regular function.

Ex3_1: Lambda with Default Parameter. Live code @Wandbox

```
#include <iostream>

int main() {
    const auto lam = [](int x = 10) { std::cout << x << '\n'; };
    lam();
    lam(100);
}
```

In the above example, we call the lambda twice. The first time without any arguments, and then it uses a default value x = 10. The second time we pass 100.

What's interesting is that GCC and Clang have supported this feature since C++11.

Return Type Deduction

If you remember from the previous chapter, the return type for a simple lambda could be deduced by the compiler. In C++14, this functionality was "extended" to regular functions and you can use auto as a return type:

```
auto myFunction() {
    const int x = computeX(...);
    const int y = computeY(...);
    return x + y;
}
```

Above, the compiler will deduce int as a return type.

For lambda expressions, in C++14, it means that they share the same rules as functions with auto return type. Let's see the Standard at [expr.prim.lambda#4][3]:

---

[3]https://timsong-cpp.github.io/cppwp/n4140/expr.prim.lambda#4

> The lambda return type is auto, which is replaced by the trailing-return-type if provided and/or deduced from return statements as described in dcl.spec.auto.

If you have multiple return statements they all have to deduce the same type:

```
auto foo = [] (int x) {
    if (x < 0) return x * 1.1f; // float!

    return x * 2.1;   // double!
};
```

The above code won't compile as the first return statement returns float while the second double. The compiler cannot decide, so you have to select the single type.

While deducing integers or doubles might be helpful, there are far more significant reasons why return type deduction is valuable. This functionality plays a considerable aspect with template code and things that are "unknown".

For example, the lambda closure type is anonymous, and we cannot specify it explicitly in our code. If you want to return a lambda from a function, then how do you specify the type?

Before C++14 you could use std::function:

Ex3_2: Returning std::function. Live code @Wandbox

```
#include <functional>
#include <iostream>

std::function<int(int)> CreateMulLambda(int x) {
    return [x](int param) noexcept { return x * param; };
}

int main() {
    const auto lam = CreateMulLambda(10);

    std::cout << sizeof(lam);

    return lam(2);
}
```

However, the above solution is not straightforward. It requires you to specify the function signature and even include some extra header file `<functional>`. If you recall from the C++11 chapter, `std::function` is a heavy object (in GCC 9 the `sizeof` shows 32 bytes) and it needs some advanced internal mechanics so that it can handle any callable objects.

Thanks to the improvements in C++14, we can now simplify the code:

Ex3_3: Auto return type deduction for lambdas. Live code @Wandbox

```cpp
#include <iostream>

auto CreateMulLambda(int x) noexcept {
    return [x](int param) noexcept { return x * param; };
}

int main() {
    const auto lam = CreateMulLambda(10);

    std::cout << sizeof(lam);

    return lam(2);
}
```

This time we can entirely rely on the compile-time type deduction, and no helper types are required. On GCC the size of lambda `sizeof(lam)` is just 4 bytes and it's far cheaper than the solution with `std::function`. Please notice that we could also mark `CreateMulLambda` with `noexcept` as there no way it can throw any exception. This was not the case when returning `std::function`.

Captures With an Initialiser

Now some more significant updates!

As you recall, in a lambda expression you can capture variables from the outside scope. The compiler expands that capture syntax and creates corresponding non-static data members in the closure type.

Now, in C++14, you can create new data members and initialise them in the capture clause. Then you can access those variables inside the lambda. It's called *capture with an initialiser* or another name for this feature is *generalised lambda capture.*

For example:

Ex3_4: Capture With an Initialiser. Live code @Wandbox

```
#include <iostream>

int main() {
    int x = 30;
    int y = 12;
    const auto foo = [z = x + y]() { std::cout << z << '\n'; };
    x = 0;
    y = 0;
    foo();
}
```

The output:

42

In the example above, the compiler generates a new data member and initialises it with x+y. The type of the new variable is deduced in the same way as if you put auto in front of this new variable. In our case:

```
auto z = x + y;
```

In summary, the lambda from the preceding example resolves into a following (simplified) callable type:

```
struct _unnamedLambda {
    void operator()() const {
        std::cout << z << '\n';
    }

    int z;
} someInstance;
```

z will be directly initialised (with x+y) when the lambda expression is defined.

Keep in mind the previous sentence. The new variable is initialised at the place where you define a lambda and not where you invoke it.

That's why if you modify the x or y variables after you created the lambda, the variable z won't change. In the example, you can see that immediately after the lambda was defined I changed the values of x and y. Yet the output will be still 42 as z was initialised earlier.

Creating variables through an initialiser is also flexible since you can, for example, create references to variables from the outside scope.

Ex3_5: Reference as Capture With an Initialiser. Live code @Wandbox

```cpp
#include <iostream>

int main() {
    int x = 30;
    const auto foo = [&z = x]() { std::cout << z << '\n'; };
    foo();
    x = 0;
    foo();
}
```

This time the z variable is a reference to x. It's created in the same way as you'd write:

```cpp
auto &z = x;
```

If you run the example, you should see that the first line prints 30, but the second line shows 0. This is because we captured a reference so when you modify the referenced variable, the z object will also change.

Limitations

Please note that while you can capture by reference with an initialiser, it's not possible to write r-value reference &&. That's why the below code is invalid:

```cpp
[&&z = x] // invalid syntax!
```

Another limitation for the feature is that it doesn't allow parameter packs. Let's have a look at the section 24 of [expr.prim.lambda][4]:

---

[4]https://timsong-cpp.github.io/cppwp/n4140/expr.prim.lambda#24

A simple-capture followed by an ellipsis is a pack expansion ([temp.variadic]). An init-capture followed by an ellipsis is ill-formed.

In other words, in C++14, you cannot write:

```
template<class... Args>
auto captureTest(Args... args) {
    return lambda = [...capturedArgs = std::move(args)](){};
    // ...
```

This syntax, however, will be possible with C++20, see in this section on page 114.

Improvements for Existing Issues

The new C++14 functionality of a capture with an initialiser can solve a few problems, for example with movable-only types or allow some extra optimisation.

Let's review them now.

Move

Previously in C++11, you couldn't capture a unique pointer by value. Only capturing by reference was possible. Now, since C++14, we can move an object into a member of the closure type:

Ex3_6: Capturing a movable only type. Live code @Wandbox

```
#include <iostream>
#include <memory>

int main(){
    std::unique_ptr<int> p(new int{10});
    const auto bar = [ptr=std::move(p)] {
        std::cout << "pointer in lambda: " << ptr.get() << '\n';
    };
    std::cout << "pointer in main(): " << p.get() << '\n';
    bar();
}
```

The output:

```
pointer in main(): 0
pointer in lambda: 0x1413c20
```

Thanks to the capture initialiser you can move the pointer ownership into the lambda. As you can see in the example, the unique pointer is set to nullptr just after the closure object is created. But when you call a lambda, then you'll see a valid memory address.

One Gotcha with std::function

Having a moveable-only captured variable in a lambda makes the closure object not copyable. This might be an issue if you want to store such a lambda in std::function which accepts only copyable callable objects.

We can observe this in detail if we run C++Insights on the previous example (see this link for a live code[5]). You will see that std::unique_ptr is a data member of the closure type, and having a moveable-only member prevents the compiler from creating a default copy constructor.

In short, this code won't compile:

Ex3_7: **std::function** and **std::move**. Live code @Wandbox

```
std::unique_ptr<int> p(new int{10});
std::function<void()> fn = [ptr = std::move(p)]() { }; // won't compile!
```

 If you want the full details you can also have a look at the proposal of any_-invocable (P0288[6]) which is a possible future improvement for std::function and also handles moveable-only types.

Optimisation

Another idea is to use capture initialisers as a potential optimisation technique. Rather than computing some value every time we invoke a lambda, we can compute it once in the initialiser:

---

[5]https://cppinsights.io/s/5d11eb8f
[6]https://wg21.link/P0288

Ex3_8: Creating a string for a lambda. Live code @Wandbox

```cpp
#include <algorithm>
#include <iostream>
#include <string>
#include <vector>

int main() {
    using namespace std::string_literals;
    const std::vector<std::string> vs = { "apple", "orange",
                                          "foobar", "lemon" };

    const auto prefix = "foo"s;

    auto result = std::find_if(vs.begin(), vs.end(),
        [&prefix](const std::string& s) {
            return s == prefix + "bar"s;
        }
    );
    if (result != vs.end())
        std::cout << prefix << "-something found!\n";

    result = std::find_if(vs.begin(), vs.end(),
        [savedString = prefix + "bar"s](const std::string& s) {
            return s == savedString;
        }
    );
    if (result != vs.end())
        std::cout << prefix << "-something found!\n";
}
```

The code above shows two calls to std::find_if. In the first scenario, we capture prefix and compare the input value against prefix + "bar"s. Every time the lambda is invoked a temporary value that stores the sum of those strings has to be created and computed.

The second call to find_if shows an optimisation: we create a captured variable savedString that computes the sum of strings. Then, we can safely refer to it in the lambda body. The sum of strings will run only once and not with every invocation of the lambda.

The example also uses `std::string_literals`, and that's why we can write `"foo"s` which represents a `std::string` object.

Capturing a Class Data Member

An initialiser can also be used to capture data members without worrying about `*this` pointer. We can capture a copy of a data member and don't bother with dangling references.

For example:

Ex3_9: Capturing a data member. Live code @Wandbox

```
#include <algorithm>
#include <iostream>

struct Baz {
    auto foo() const {
        return [s=s] { std::cout << s << '\n'; };
    }

    std::string s;
};

int main() {
    const auto f1 = Baz{"abc"}.foo();
    const auto f2 = Baz{"xyz"}.foo();
    f1();
    f2();
}
```

In `foo()` we capture a data member by copying it into the closure type. Additionally, we use `auto` for the deduction of the return type of the member function `foo()`. As a remark, in C++11, we would have to use `std::function`, see in the C++11 chapter on page 31.

It might be surprising that we used a "strange" syntax like `[s = s]` when declaring the lambda. This code works because a captured variable is in the scope of the closure type and not in the outside scope. That's why there's no conflict here.

Generic Lambdas

That's a big one!

The early specification of lambda expressions allowed us to create anonymous function objects (closure types) and pass them to various generic algorithms from the Standard Library. However, closures were not "generic" on their own. For example, you couldn't specify a template parameter as a lambda parameter.

Fortunately, since C++14, the Standard introduced *Generic Lambdas* and now we can write:

```cpp
const auto foo = [](auto x, int y) { std::cout << x << ", " y << '\n'; };
foo(10, 1);
foo(10.1234, 2);
foo("hello world", 3);
```

Please notice `auto x` as a parameter to the lambda. This is equivalent to using a template declaration in the call operator of the closure type:

```cpp
struct {
    template<typename T>
    void operator()(T x, int y) const {
        std::cout << x << ", " y << '\n';
    }
} someInstance;
```

If there are more `auto` arguments, then the code expands to separate template parameters:

```cpp
const auto fooDouble = [](auto x, auto y) { /*...*/ };
```

Expands into:

```cpp
struct {
    template<typename T, typename U>
    void operator()(T x, U y) const { /*...*/ }
} someOtherInstance;
```

Variadic Generic Arguments

But that's not all. If you need more function parameters, then you can also go "variadic":

For example:

Ex3_10: Generic Variadic Lambda, Sum. Live code @Wandbox

```cpp
#include <iostream>

template<typename T>
auto sum(T x) { return x; }

template<typename T1, typename... T>
auto sum(T1 s, T... ts) { return s + sum(ts...); }

int main() {
    const auto sumLambda = [] (auto... args) {
        std::cout << "sum of: " << sizeof...(args) << " numbers\n";
        return sum(args...);
    };

    std::cout << sumLambda(1.1, 2.2, 3.3, 4.4, 5.5, 6.6, 7.7, 8.8, 9.9 );
}
```

In the above sample the generic lambda uses auto... to represent a variadic argument pack. Conceptually it's expanded into the following call operator:

```cpp
struct __anonymousLambda{
    template<typename... T>
    void operator()(T... args) const { /*...*/ }
};
```

> In C++17 we got fold expressions which can improve generic variadic lambdas, and in C++20 we'll get more control over the template arguments. For more information see C++17's updates to variadic generic lambdas (page 91), and also in C++20 about template lambdas (page 115).

Perfect Forwarding with Generic Lambdas

With generic lambdas you're not restricted to using auto x, you can add any qualifiers as with other auto variables like auto&, const auto& or auto&&. One of the handy use cases is that you can specify auto&& x which becomes a forwarding (universal) reference. This allows you to perfectly forward the input arguments:

Ex3_11: Perfect Forwarding with Generic Lambda. Live code @Wandbox

```cpp
#include <iostream>
#include <string>

void foo(const std::string& ) { std::cout << "foo(const string&)\n"; }
void foo(std::string&& ) { std::cout << "foo(string&&)\n"; }

int main() {
    const auto callFoo = [](auto &&str) {
        std::cout << "Calling foo() on: " << str << '\n';
        foo(std::forward<decltype(str)>(str));
    };

    const std::string str = "Hello World";
    callFoo(str);
    callFoo("Hello World Ref Ref");
}
```

The output:

```
Calling foo() on: Hello World
foo(const string&)
Calling foo() on: Hello World Ref Ref
foo(string&&)
```

The sample code defines two function overloads foo for const references to std::string and one for r-value references to std::string. The callFoo lambda uses a generic argument that is a universal reference[7]. If you wanted to rewrite this lambda into a regular function template it could look like:

---

[7]You can read more about universal references in this article from Scott Meyers: Universal References in C++11

```
template <typename T>
void callFooFunc(T&& str) {
    std::cout << "Calling foo() on: " << str << '\n';
    foo(std::forward<T>(str));
}
```

As you can see with generic lambdas, you have more options to write local anonymous functions.

But there's more.

Deducing the Correct Type

Additionally, generic lambdas might be very helpful when type deduction is tricky.

For example:

Ex3_12: Correct type for map iteration. Live code @Wandbox

```
#include <algorithm>
#include <iostream>
#include <map>
#include <string>

int main() {
    const std::map<std::string, int> numbers {
        { "one", 1 }, {"two", 2 }, { "three", 3 }
    };

    // each time entry is copied from pair<const string, int>!
    std::for_each(std::begin(numbers), std::end(numbers),
        [](const std::pair<std::string, int>& entry) {
            std::cout << entry.first << " = " << entry.second << '\n';
        }
    );
}
```

Did I make any mistake here? Does entry have the correct type?

The code is wrong as the value type for `std::map` is `std::pair<const Key, T>` and not `const std::pair<Key, T>`. For our case, the code performed extra copies due to the conversion between `std::pair<const std::string, int>` and `const std::pair<std::string, int>&` (ie. `const std::string` to `std::string`):

This can be fixed by using `auto`:

```cpp
std::for_each(std::begin(numbers), std::end(numbers),
    [](const auto& entry) {
        std::cout << entry.first << " = " << entry.second << '\n';
    }
);
```

Now the template argument deduction will correctly get the correct type of the `entry` object, and there will be no additional copy created. Not to mention the code is much easier to read and shorter.

See the full example which also contains code that prints the addresses of the entries:

Ex3_13: Correct type for map iteration, full version. Live code @Wandbox

```cpp
#include <algorithm>
#include <iostream>
#include <map>
#include <string>

int main() {
    const std::map<std::string, int> numbers {
        { "one", 1 }, {"two", 2 }, { "three", 3 }
    };

    // print addresses:
    for (auto mit = numbers.cbegin(); mit != numbers.cend(); ++mit)
        std::cout << &mit->first << ", " << &mit->second << '\n';

    // each time entry is copied from pair<const string, int>!
    std::for_each(std::begin(numbers), std::end(numbers),
        [](const std::pair<std::string, int>& entry) {
            std::cout << &entry.first << ", " << &entry.second << ": "
                      << entry.first << " = " << entry.second << '\n';
        }
```

```
    );

    // this time entries are not copied, they have the same addresses
    std::for_each(std::begin(numbers), std::end(numbers),
        [](const auto& entry) {
            std::cout << &entry.first << ", " << &entry.second << ": "
                      << entry.first << " = " << entry.second << '\n';
        }
    );
}
```

And here's a possible output:

```
1  0x165dc40, 0x165dc60
2  0x165dce0, 0x165dd00
3  0x165dc90, 0x165dcb0
4  0x7ffe5ed29a20, 0x7ffe5ed29a40: one = 1
5  0x7ffe5ed29a20, 0x7ffe5ed29a40: three = 3
6  0x7ffe5ed29a20, 0x7ffe5ed29a40: two = 2
7  0x165dc40, 0x165dc60: one = 1
8  0x165dce0, 0x165dd00: three = 3
9  0x165dc90, 0x165dcb0: two = 2
```

The first three lines show the addresses of keys and values from the map. Later in lines 4, 5 and 6, you can see three new addresses which are the same, but they are probably temporary copies for the loop iteration. The last three lines illustrate the version with const auto&, and as you can notice, the addresses are the same as in the first three lines.

In our example, we focused on extra copies of keys, but it's vital to understand that also the value entry is copied. This might not be an issue when you use a cheap-to-copy type like int, but it might cost much more if the objects are larger like strings.

 In C++20 you'll get even more control over the template argument for lambdas as this new revision of C++ introduces template lambdas, concepts and constrained auto parameters.

Replacing `std::bind1st` and `std::bind2nd` with Lambdas

In the chapter about C++98/03, I mentioned and showed a few code samples with functional helpers like `std::bind1st` and `std::bind2nd`. However, since C++11 the functionality became deprecated, and in C++17, the functions were removed.

Functions like `bind1st()`/`bind2nd()`/`mem_fun()`, … were introduced in the C++98-era and are not needed now as you can apply a lambda or use modern alternatives. What's more, the routines were not updated to handle perfect forwarding, variadic templates, `decltype` and other techniques from C++11. Thus it's best not to use them in modern code.

Here's the list of deprecated functionality:

- `unary_function()/pointer_to_unary_function()`
- `binary_function()/pointer_to_binary_function()`
- `bind1st()/binder1st`
- `bind2nd()/binder2nd`
- `ptr_fun()`
- `mem_fun()`
- `mem_fun_ref()`

To replace `bind1st/bind2nd` you can use lambdas or `std::bind` (available since C++11) or `std::bind_front` (since C++20).

Let's consider the following code which uses the old functionality:

```
const auto onePlus = std::bind1st(std::plus<int>(), 1);
const auto minusOne = std::bind2nd(std::minus<int>(), 1);
std::cout << onePlus(10) << ", " << minusOne(10) << '\n';
```

In the preceding example, `onePlus` is a callable object composed of `std::plus` with the first argument fixed. In other words when you write `onePlus(n)` it's then "expanded" into `std::plus(1, n)`.

Similarly, `minusOne` is a composed of `std::minus` with the second argument fixed to one. Thus `minusOne(n)` "expands" into `std::minus(n, 1)`.

The above syntax is quite complicated, so let's see how it can be improved with Modern C++ patterns.

Using Modern C++ Techniques

Let's try with `std::bind` - which offers more flexibility than `bind1st` or `bind2nd`.

Ex3_14: Replacing with **std::bind**. Live code @Compiler Explorer

```
#include <algorithm>
#include <functional>
#include <iostream>

int main() {
    using std::placeholders::_1;
    const auto onePlus = std::bind(std::plus<int>(), _1, 1);
    const auto minusOne = std::bind(std::minus<int>(), 1, _1);
    std::cout << onePlus(10) << ", " << minusOne(10) << '\n';
}
```

`std::bind` is more flexible as it can support multiple arguments or can even reorder them. For argument management, you need to use "placeholders". In our example, we used `_1` to represent the first argument that will be passed to the final function object.

While `std::bind` is much better than the C++98/03 legacy helpers, it's still not as natural as lambda expressions.

We can write at least two versions with lambdas. The first one with the hardcoded values for the operations:

```
auto lamOnePlus1 = [](int b) { return 1 + b; };
auto lamMinusOne1 = [](int b) { return b - 1; };
std::cout << lamOnePlus1(10) << ", " << lamMinusOne1(10) << '\n';
```

Still, since C++14 we can also take advantage of capture with initialiser and be more flexible:

```
auto lamOnePlus = [a=1](int b) { return a + b; };
auto lamMinusOne = [a=1](int b) { return b - a; };
std::cout << lamOnePlus(10) << ", " << lamMinusOne(10) << '\n';
```

The lambda version is much cleaner and more readable. This will be more visible in a more complicated example below.

Function Composition

As a final example let's have a look at the following code with function composition:

Ex3_15: Function composition with std::bind. Live code @Compiler Explorer

```cpp
#include <algorithm>
#include <functional>
#include <vector>

int main() {
    using std::placeholders::_1;

    const std::vector<int> v { 1, 2, 3, 4, 5, 6, 7, 8, 9 };
    const auto val = std::count_if(v.begin(), v.end(),
                            std::bind(std::logical_and<bool>(),
                            std::bind(std::greater<int>(), _1, 2),
                            std::bind(std::less<int>(), _1, 6)));

    return val;
}
```

Can you immediately decipher what's going on there[8]?

And now let's rewrite this complicated composition with a simple lambda expression:

```cpp
const std::vector<int> v { 1, 2, 3, 4, 5, 6, 7, 8, 9 };
const auto more2less6 = std::count_if(v.begin(), v.end(),
                            [](int x) { return x > 2 && x < 6;});
```

Isn't that better?

 You can read more about the guidelines for the use of std::bind and lambdas in the following resources: in "Effective Modern C++", Item 34: Prefer lambdas to std::bind, and on the Google Abseil Blog: Tip of the Week #108: Avoid std::bind[9].

---

[8]I used val as a vague name on purpose, so its meaning is not clear.
[9]https://abseil.io/tips/108

LIFTing with lambdas

While the algorithms from the Standard Library are convenient, some issues are hard to solve. One of them is passing function overloads into function templates that takes a callable object.

For example:

Calling function overloads

```cpp
#include <algorithm>
#include <vector>

// two overloads:
void foo(int) {}
void foo(float) {}

int main() {
    const std::vector<int> vi { 1, 2, 3, 4, 5, 6, 7, 8, 9 };
    std::for_each(vi.begin(), vi.end(), foo);
}
```

In the above example, we try to use foo which has two overloads for int and float and pass it into for_each. Unfortunately, we get the following error from GCC 9 (trunk):

```
error: no matching function for call to
for_each(std::vector<int>::iterator, std::vector<int>::iterator,
 <unresolved overloaded function type>)
    std::for_each(vi.begin(), vi.end(), foo);
                                        ^^^^^
```

The main issue here is that the compiler sees foo as a template parameter, so it needs to resolve its type. But to do this it would have to check what types foo accepts, which is not possible.

However, there's a trick where we can use a lambda and then call the desired function overload.

In a basic form, for simple value types, for our two functions, we can write the following code:

```
std::for_each(vi.begin(), vi.end(), [](auto x) { return foo(x); });
```

Now, we have a wrapper (a generic lambda) which handles the overload resolution and calls the proper overload for `foo()`.

We can improve this by using perfect forwarding:

```
std::for_each(vi.begin(), vi.end(), [](auto&& x) {
    return foo(std::forward<decltype>(x)>(x); }
);
```

And here's the working example:

Ex3_16: Generic Lambda and Function Overload. Live code @Wandbox

```
#include <algorithm>
#include <iostream>
#include <vector>

void foo(int i) { std::cout << "int: " << i << "\n"; }
void foo(float f) { std::cout << "float: " << f << "\n"; }

int main() {
    const std::vector<int> vi { 1, 2, 3, 4, 5, 6, 7, 8, 9 };
    std::for_each(vi.begin(), vi.end(), [](auto&& x) {
        return foo(std::forward<decltype>(x)>(x));
    });
}
```

However, for more advanced scenarios, this might not be a preferred solution. It's because we don't honour variadic arguments and exception specifications.

If you need a more generic, and better solution, then you need to write a bit more code:

```
#define LIFT(foo) \
  [](auto&&... x) \
    noexcept(noexcept(foo(std::forward<decltype(x)>(x)...))) \
   -> decltype(foo(std::forward<decltype(x)>(x)...)) \
  { return foo(std::forward<decltype(x)>(x)...); }
```

Quite complicated code... right? :)

Let's try to decipher it. There are three duplicated parts:

- `return foo(std::forward<decltype(x)>(x)...);` - this is perfect forwarding so that we can properly pass input arguments into the `foo` function preserving their types.
- `noexcept(noexcept(foo(std::forward<decltype(x)>(x)...)))` - uses the `noexcept` operator (the nested one) to check the exception specification of the `foo` callable object. Depending on the result it will yield `noexcept(true)` or `noexcept(false)`.
- `decltype(foo(std::forward<decltype(x)>(x)...)` it's used to deduce the return type for the wrapper lambda

`LIFT` is defined as a macro as otherwise you'd have to write this code every time you'd like to create such lambda and pass it into an algorithm. In this case, macros are the easiest syntax we can use[10].

Play with the final code @Wandbox[11].

Recursive Lambdas

If you have a regular function then it's easy to call it recursively. But is the same possible with lambda expressions? Let's see.

A common example for a recursion is the calculation of a factorial. Here's an example with a regular function:

---

[10]. For more information and proposals on how to improve the syntax, you can read this blog post *Passing overload sets to functions* by Sy Brand.

[11]https://wandbox.org/permlink/r81jASiPPmYXTOmx

Ex3_17: Recursion with a Regular Function. Live code @Wandbox

```cpp
int factorial(int n) {
    return n > 1 ? n * factorial(n - 1) : 1;
}

int main() {
    return factorial(5);
}
```

However it's not directly possible with lambdas:

Ex3_18: Errors with Recursive Lambda. Live code @Wandbox

```cpp
int main() {
    auto factorial = [](int n) {
        return n > 1 ? n * factorial(n - 1) : 1;
    };
    return factorial(5);
}
```

This code doesn't compile! Here's an error from GCC:

```
error: use of 'factorial' before deduction of 'auto'
```

This happens because we cannot access `factorial` inside a body of the lambda, as it's still not fully evaluated. To illustrate this issue we can "expand" the code into a simplified function object type:

```cpp
struct fact {
    int operator()(int n) const {
        return n > 1 ? n * factorial(n - 1) : 1;
    };
};

auto factorial = fact{};
```

As you can see, inside `operator()` there's no way we can access a variable of the callable type.

If you need to call a lambda recursively, there are at least two tricks that you can leverage:

- With `std::function` and capturing it.
- With an internal lambda and passing it as a generic parameter.

Let's see the first option:

With `std::function`

The main idea is that we can assign a lambda to `std::function`[12] and then we can capture this object into the lambda body.

Ex3_19: Recursive Lambda with `std::function`. Live code @Wandbox

```cpp
#include <functional>

int main() {
    const std::function<int(int)> factorial = [&factorial](int n) {
        return n > 1 ? n * factorial(n - 1) : 1;
    };
    return factorial(5);
}
```

In the previous code sample, inside the lambda body, we call `factorial` which is a captured `std::function` object. This object is fully defined, and that's why the compiler has no issues when accessing and calling it.

If you want to use only stateless lambdas, then you might even try with a function pointer rather than `std::function` as it should cost much less memory.

But there's one more trick:

Internal Lambda and a Generic Parameter

With C++14 we can use the following alternative:

---

[12]We discussed assigning to `std::function` in the "The Type of a Lambda Expression" in the C++11 chapter.

Ex3_20: Recursive Lambda with internal implementation. Live code @Wandbox

```cpp
int main() {
    const auto factorial = [](int n) noexcept {
        const auto f_impl = [](int n, const auto& impl) noexcept -> int {
            return n > 1 ? n * impl(n - 1, impl) : 1;
        };
        return f_impl(n, f_impl);
    };
    return factorial(5);
}
```

This time we create an internal lambda that performs the primary processing (f_impl). Later, we pass a generic argument to it (const auto& impl). This parameter is a callable object that we can call recursively. Thanks to generic lambdas in C++14 we can avoid the cost of std::function and rely on auto type deduction.

More Tricks

If you'd like to see more tricks, then you can also have a look at the following resources:

- c++ - Recursive lambda functions in C++11 - Stack Overflow[13]
- Recursive lambdas in C++(14) - Pedro Melendez[14]

Is a recursive lambda the best alternative?

In this section, you could see some of the tricks with the lambda expression. Nevertheless, the complexity of those techniques is way over a simple solution with just a recursive function call. That's why there might be cases where a recursive lambda is not the best and the most straightforward option. On the other hand, the strong points for complicated recursive lambdas are its locality and the ability to take auto arguments.

---

[13]https://stackoverflow.com/questions/2067988/recursive-lambda-functions-in-c11
[14]http://pedromelendez.com/blog/2015/07/16/recursive-lambdas-in-c14/

Summary

As you saw in this chapter, C++14 brought several key improvements to lambda expressions. Since C++14 you can now declare new variables to use inside a lambda scope, and you can also use them efficiently in template code. In the next chapter, we'll dive into C++17, which brings more updates!

4. Lambdas in C++17

C++17 added two significant enhancements to lambda expressions:

- `constexpr` lambdas
- Capture of `*this`

The new C++ revision also updated the type system - it now contains an exception specification, which also relates to lambda expressions.

You can see the specification related to lambdas in N659[1] (C++17 draft just before publication) and the lambda section: [expr.prim.lambda][2].

Additionally, you'll learn about the following techniques:

- How to improve the IIFE pattern in C++17.
- How to improve variadic generic lambdas with fold expressions from C++17.
- How to derive from multiple lambdas.
- Lambdas and Asynchronous Execution.

Let's start!

---

[1]https://timsong-cpp.github.io/cppwp/n4659/
[2]https://timsong-cpp.github.io/cppwp/n4659/expr.prim.lambda

Lambda Syntax Update

With C++17, we have a few changes to the syntax of lambda expressions:

- You can now add `constexpr` after the parameter list.
- The dynamic exception specification was deprecated in C++11 and removed in C++17, so in practice, you should only use `noexcept`.

See an updated diagram below:

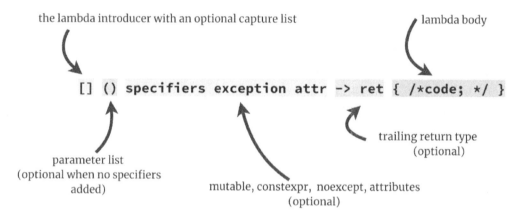

Lambda Syntax in C++17

You can read about this new modification in the next section.

Exception Specification in the Type System

Before we move to syntax improvements for lambdas, we need to cover one "general" language feature that was introduced into C++17.

The exception specification for a function didn't use to belong to the type of the function, but now, in C++17, it's part of it. This means you can have two function overloads: one with `noexcept` and the second without it. See below:

Ex4_1: Exception Specification in the Type System. Live code @Wandbox

```cpp
using TNoexceptVoidFunc = void (*)() noexcept;
void SimpleNoexceptCall(TNoexceptVoidFunc f) { f(); }

using TVoidFunc = void (*)();
void SimpleCall(TVoidFunc f) { f(); }

void fNoexcept() noexcept { }
void fRegular() { }

int main() {
    SimpleNoexceptCall(fNoexcept);
    SimpleNoexceptCall([]() noexcept { });
    // SimpleNoexceptCall(fRegular);    // cannot convert
    // SimpleNoexceptCall([]() { });    // cannot convert

    SimpleCall(fNoexcept); // converts to regular function
    SimpleCall(fRegular);
    SimpleCall([]() noexcept { });    // converts
    SimpleCall([]() { });
}
```

A pointer to a noexcept function can be converted to a pointer to a regular function (this also works for a pointer to a member function and also for lambdas). But it's not possible the other way around (from a regular function pointer into a function pointer that is marked with noexcept).

One of the reasons for adding the feature is a chance to optimise the code better. If the compiler has a guarantee that a function won't throw, then it can potentially generate faster code (see Why can noexcept generate faster code than throw()? @Standard C++[3]). Inside the Standard Library, there are many places where noexcept is checked and based on that the code can be more efficient. This is how it works for std::vector which can differentiate between stored types that can move without throwing or not.

Here's an example which uses type traits and if constexpr to check if a given callable object is marked with noexcept:

---

[3]https://isocpp.org/blog/2014/09/noexcept-optimization

```cpp
#include <iostream>
#include <type_traits>

template<typename Callable>
void CallWith10(Callable&& fn) {
    if constexpr (std::is_nothrow_invocable_v<Callable, int>) {
        std::cout << "Calling fn(10) with optimisation\n";
        fn(10);
    }
    else {
        std::cout << "Calling fn(10) normally\n";
        fn(10);
    }
}

int main() {
    int x {10};
    const auto lam = [&x](int y) noexcept { x += y; };
    CallWith10(lam);

    const auto lamEx = [&x](int y) {
        std::cout << "lamEx with x = " << x << '\n';
        x += y;
    };
    CallWith10(lamEx);
}
```

The output:

```
Calling fn(10) with optimisation
Calling fn(10) normally
lamEx with x = 20
```

The code uses std::is_nothrow_invocable_v to check if the given callable object is marked with noexcept.

In C++17, the Exception Specification is cleaned up. Effectively, you can only use noexcept for declaring that a function won't throw. The dynamic exception specification, i.e. throw(X, Y, Z) is now removed.

Quick Question: What happens if you mark a function with `noexcept` and yet it throws an exception? In that case, the compiler will call `std::terminate`.

`constexpr` Lambda Expressions

Since C++11, `constexpr` has allowed more and more code to be evaluated at compile time. This not only affects the performance but more importantly makes compile-time coding much more pleasant and potent. In C++17, this powerful keyword can also be applied on lambdas Let's see the specification expr.prim.lambda #4[4]:

> The function call operator is a `constexpr` function if either the corresponding lambda-expression's parameter-declaration-clause is followed by `constexpr`, or it satisfies the requirements for a `constexpr` function.

In other words, if the lambda body follows the rules of a `constexpr` function then, `operator()` for the closure type is implicitly defined as `constexpr`. To recall, in C++17, a `constexpr` function has the following rules n4659/dcl.constexpr#3[5]:

- it shall not be virtual;
- its return type shall be a literal type;
- each of its parameter types shall be a literal type;
- its function-body shall be = `delete`, = `default`, or a compound-statement that does not contain
  - an `asm`-definition,
  - a goto statement,
  - an identifier label,
  - a try-block, or
  - a definition of a variable of non-literal type or of static or thread storage duration or for which no initialisation is performed.

---

[4]https://timsong-cpp.github.io/cppwp/n4659/expr.prim.lambda#closure-4
[5]https://timsong-cpp.github.io/cppwp/n4659/dcl.constexpr#3

For example:

```
constexpr auto Square = [](int n) { return n * n; }; // implicit constexpr
static_assert(Square(2) == 4);
```

Since the body of Square is simple and it doesn't violate constexpr rules, then it's implicitly marked as constexpr and we can call it at compile-time with static_assert.

Examples

How about more practical code samples? At start, let's consider an implementation of a popular numerical algorithm:

Ex4_3: **constexpr** lambda - Simple Accumulate. **Live code @Wandbox**

```
#include <array>

template<typename Range, typename Func, typename T>
constexpr T SimpleAccumulate(Range&& range, Func func, T init) {
    for (auto &&elem: range) {
        init += func(elem);
    }
    return init;
}

int main() {
    constexpr std::array arr{ 1, 2, 3 };

    constexpr auto sum = SimpleAccumulate(arr, [](auto i) {
            return i * i;
        }, 0);

    static_assert(sum == 14);
}
```

The code uses a constexpr lambda which is passed to SimpleAccumulate. The lambda is not explicitly marked with constexpr, but the compiler will declare its call operator with constexpr as the body contains just a simple computation. The algorithm also uses a few

C++17 elements: constexpr additions to std::array, std::begin and std::end (used in range-based for-loop) are now also constexpr so it means that the whole code might be executed at compile time.

As another example we can use and enhance a recursive lambda from the C++14 chapter (page 73):

Ex4_4: Recursive **constexpr** Lambda. Live code @Compiler Explorer

```
int main() {
    constexpr auto factorial = [](int n) {
        constexpr auto fact_impl = [](int n, const auto& impl) -> int {
            return n > 1 ? n * impl(n - 1, impl) : 1;
        };
        return fact_impl(n, fact_impl);
    };
    static_assert(factorial(5) == 120);
}
```

In the example, we marked the factorial with constexpr, and this allows checking the computation through static_assert. Have a look at the live code at Compiler Explorer to see the generated assembler - it's almost "no-op" even with disabled optimisation level.

Capturing Variables

You can also capture variables (assuming they are also constant expressions):

Ex4_5: Capturing a **constexpr** variable. Live code @Wandbox

```
constexpr int add(int const& t, int const& u) { return t + u; }

int main() {
    constexpr int x = 0;
    constexpr auto lam = [x](int n) { return add(x, n); };

    static_assert(lam(10) == 10);
}
```

However, there's an interesting case where you don't "pass" a captured variable any further, like:

```
constexpr int x = 0;
constexpr auto lam = [x](int n) { return n + x; };
```

In that case, in Clang, we might get the following warning:

```
warning: lambda capture 'x' is not required to be captured for this use
```

The same happens when we change the implementation of add() so it takes arguments by value:

```
constexpr int add(int t, int u) { return t + u; }
```

It's because if we rely on constant expressions the compiler can optimise away the variables, especially for built-in types for which we know the values at compile-time.

Here's some extra description from cppreference[6]:

> A lambda expression can read the value of a variable without capturing it if the variable
>
> - has const non-volatile integral or enumeration type and has been initialised with a constant expression, or
> - is constexpr and has no mutable members.

For more information you can also read this part of the Standard: C++ draft - basic.def.odr#4[7].

In the first add() example, that took a variable by reference, we enforce the compiler to create a closure member that can be then bound to the reference. Imagine that the add() function returns the address of the argument and then it will be compared against x, like so:

---

[6]https://en.cppreference.com/w/cpp/language/lambda
[7]https://eel.is/c++draft/basic.def.odr#4

```
int const* address(int const& x) {
    return &x;
}

auto f = [x] {
  auto* p = address(x);
  return p == &x; // these need to be true
};
```

Thus the compiler needs to store a copy of x inside the closure - i.e. capture it. And in this case the capture cannot be optimised away.

constexpr **Summary:**

In a nutshell:

constexpr lambdas allow you to blend with template programming and possibly have shorter code.

Be prepared for the future:

In C++20 we'll have lots of constexpr standard algorithms and containers like std::vector and std::string, so constexpr lambdas will be very handy in that context. Your code will look the same for the runtime version as well as for constexpr (compile-time) version!

Let's now move to the second important feature available since C++17:

Capture of *this

Do you remember the issue when we wanted to capture a class member[8]?

By default, we capture this (as a pointer!), and that's why we might get into trouble when temporary objects go out of scope.

In C++17 we have another way. We can capture a copy of *this[9]:

---

[8]See in the C++11 Chapter - Capturing a Class Member on page 31.
[9]To capture *this, the class has to be copyable. You can't use *this to capture a move-only class.

Ex4_6: Capturing *this. Live code @Wandbox

```cpp
#include <iostream>

struct Baz {
    auto foo() {
        return [*this] { std::cout << s << '\n'; };
    }

    std::string s;
};

int main() {
    const auto f1 = Baz{"xyz"}.foo();
    const auto f2 = Baz{"abc"}.foo();
    f1();
    f2();
}
```

In the example we can now write [*this] which means that the lambda captures a copy of the temporary object, a copy of *this. The copy is then saved in the closure object and then there won't be any undefined behaviour when invoking the lambda later.

 Please note that in C++17 if you write [=] in a member function, then this is implicitly captured! Have a look at the C++20 Chapter when this is enhanced and deprecated! See P0806[10].

Some Guides

OK, so should we capture [this] or [*this], and why is this important?

In most cases, when you work inside the scope of a class, then [this] (or [&]) is perfectly fine. There's no extra copy which is essential when your objects are large.

You might consider [*this] when you really want a copy, and when there's a chance a lambda will outlive the object.

---

[10]https://wg21.link/P0806

This might be crucial for avoiding data races in async or parallel execution. Also, in the async/multithreading execution mode, the lambda might outlive the object, and then this pointer might no longer be alive.

Updates To IIFE

In the chapter about C++11 changes, on page 42, you learned about IIFE - Immediately Invoked Functional Expression. In C++17 there's an update to that technique.

One of the issues with IIFE is that it's sometimes hard to read, as the call syntax might be easily skipped when reading the code:

```
const auto var = [&] {
    if (TheFirstCondition())
        return one_value;

    if (TheSecondCondition())
        return second_val;

    return default_value;
}(); // call it!
```

In the C++11 chapter, we even discussed a situation where using const auto var might also be a bit misleading. It's because developers might be accustomed to the fact that var might be a closure object and not the result of the invocation.

In C++17 there's a handy template function std::invoke() that can make IIFE more visible:

```
const auto var = std::invoke([&] {
    if (TheFirstCondition())
        return one_value;

    if (TheSecondCindition())
        return second_val;

    return default_value;
});
```

As you can see, there's no need to write () at the end of the expression, and it's now clear that the code *invokes* something.

Here's another example:

Ex4_7: `std::invoke` example. Live code @Wandbox

```cpp
#include <functional> // invoke()
#include <iostream>
#include <string>

int main() {
    const std::string in { "Hello World" };
    const std::string out = std::invoke([copy = in]() mutable {
        copy.replace(copy.find("World"), 5, "C++");
        return copy;
    });
    std::cout << out;
}
```

Above, we make a copy of the in string and then replace "World" into "C++". Thanks to IIFE we can assign the computed value into a const object.

You can read more about `std::invoke` in my blog article C++20 Ranges, Projections, std::invoke and if constexpr @C++ Stories[11].

Extracting Functions with IIFE

There's also one more interesting technique that is available thanks to Lambda Expressions and IIFE. You can use it to extract code into smaller functions and make sure it's safe and compiles!

 This technique originates from a tutorial for the Jai Language[12], which was adapted and popularised among C++ programmers by Ezra (a.k.a. eracpp) via a CppCon 2019 lightning talk[13]. Jonathan Boccara also describes the technique in his blog post on Fluent C++: How Lambdas Make Function Extraction Safer[14].

[11]https://www.cppstories.com/2020/10/understanding-invoke.html/
[12]https://github.com/BSVino/JaiPrimer/blob/master/JaiPrimer.md#code-refactoring
[13]https://www.youtube.com/watch?v=VBZwzox3650
[14]https://www.fluentcpp.com/2020/11/13/how-lambdas-make-function-extraction-safer/

Suppose that you have a long code block and you have to extract it into some smaller functions. Here are the core steps:

1. Wrap the code you want to extract with IIFE and capture all by reference [&].

2. Compile the code. The compiler will complain about variables inside IIFE and not visible outside. This will be the output (return) of the IIFE.

3. Now remove "capture all by reference" and compile. The compiler will report variables that we need to pass into the lambda as parameters.

4. Create a name for the new function and copy the code from IIFE.

Here's a short example of this technique. Let's start with the following code:

Ex4_8: Student Marks. Live code @Wandbox

```cpp
#include <numeric>
#include <iostream>
#include <vector>

int main() {
    using Student = std::pair<std::vector<double>, std::string>;
    const std::vector<Student> db { { { 5.0, 5.0, 5.0, 4.0 }, "John" },
                                    { { 5.0, 5.0, 5.0, 4.0 }, "Mark" },
                                    { { 5.0, 5.0, 5.0, 4.0 }, "Jane" } };

    std::vector<std::pair<double, std::string>> averages;
    for (auto& [marks, name] : db) {
        double avg = std::accumulate(marks.begin(),
                                    marks.end(), 0.0)/marks.size();
        averages.push_back({avg, name});
    }

    for (const auto &[avg, name] : averages)
        std::cout << name << ": " << avg << '\n';
}
```

We want to extract the part about computing averages, so let's wrap the code in IIFE:

```
[&]() {
    std::vector<std::pair<double, std::string>> averages;
    for (auto& [marks, name] : db) {
        double avg = std::accumulate(marks.begin(),
                                     marks.end(), 0.0)/marks.size();
        averages.push_back({avg, name});
    }
}();
```

When we compile this we'll get an error:

```
error: 'averages' was not declared in this scope
```

It means that averages is our output from the lambda and we should return it:

```
auto averages = [&]() {
    std::vector<std::pair<double, std::string>> out;
    // compute...
    return out;
    }();
```

Now we have to remove [&] and see what are the inputs. For our case it's simple - we need db. So we can put this as an input parameter for lambda:

```
auto averages = [](const std::vector<Student>& db) {  // << param
    // rest of code is the same...
}(db); // << send param
```

And as the last step, we can now get the code and prepare the final function:

```
auto ComputeAverages(const std::vector<Student>& db) {
    std::vector<std::pair<double, std::string>> out;
    // compute...
    return out;
}
```

And call it:

```
auto averages = ComputeAverages(db);

for (const auto &[avg, name] : averages)
    std::cout << name << ": " << avg << '\n';
```

This technique makes sure that the process is safe and doesn't forget about correct inputs and output from the extracted function. Additionally, with the extracted function you can notice that the code can be even better, for example we can use some other algorithms like std::transform rather than raw loops. But let's leave that as an exercise.

Updates to Variadic Generic Lambdas

In the C++14 chapter, on page 62, we talked about the variadic argument list that we can use with generic lambdas. Thanks to fold expressions in C++17 we can write even more compact code. Here's the converted example for the sum calculation:

Ex4_9: Sum with Fold Expressions. Live code @Wandbox

```
#include <iostream>

int main() {
    const auto sumLambda = [] (auto... args) {
        std::cout << "sum of: " << sizeof...(args) << " numbers\n";
        return (args + ... + 0);
    };

    std::cout << sumLambda(1.1, 2.2, 3.3, 4.4, 5.5, 6.6, 7.7, 8.8, 9.9 );
}
```

If you compare it to the previous example from C++14, you can quickly notice that there's no need for recursion! The fold expression gives us a simple and relatively intuitive syntax for writing expressions that combines variadic arguments.

Here's another example for the variadic print utility:

Ex4_10: Simple Printer with Fold Expression. Live code @Wandbox

```
#include <iostream>

int main() {
    const auto printer = [] (auto... args) {
        (std::cout << ... << args) << '\n';
    };

    printer(1, 2, 3, "hello", 10.5f);
}
```

However, if you run the code it will print all arguments without any separator:

```
123hello10.5
```

And to solve this issue, we can introduce a little helper and also fold over comma operator rather than over <<:

Ex4_11: Printer With a Helper Internal Lambda. Live code @Wandbox

```
#include <iostream>

int main() {
    const auto printer = [] (auto... args) {
        const auto printElem = [](auto elem) {
            std::cout << elem << ", ";
        };
        (printElem(args), ...);
        std::cout << '\n';
    };

    printer(1, 2, 3, "hello", 10.5f);
}
```

And now we have the following output:

```
1, 2, 3, hello, 10.5,
```

This can be even shortened into:

```
const auto printer = [] (auto... args) {
    ((std::cout << args << ", "), ...);
    std::cout << '\n';
};
```

And if we do not want to show the last comma at the end of the print sequence we can do the following:

Ex4_12: Printing Elements Without the Last Separator. Live code @Wandbox

```
#include <iostream>

int main() {
    const auto printer = [] (auto first, auto... args) {
        std::cout << first;
        ((std::cout << ", " << args), ...);
        std::cout << '\n';
    };

    printer(1, 2, 3, "hello", 10.5f);
}
```

This time we need to use a generic template argument for the first entry and then a variadic parameter list for the rest. We can then print the first element and then add a comma before other entries. The code will now print:

```
1, 2, 3, hello, 10.5
```

Deriving from Multiple Lambdas

In the C++11 chapter, you learned about deriving from a lambda expression. While it was interesting to see such a technique, the use cases were limited.

The main issue with that approach was that it supported only a specific number of lambdas. The examples used one or two base classes. But how about using a variable number of base classes, which means a variable number of lambdas?

In C++17 we have a handy pattern for that!

Have a look:

```
template<class... Ts> struct overloaded : Ts... { using Ts::operator()...; };
template<class... Ts> overloaded(Ts...) -> overloaded<Ts...>;
```

As you can see, we need to use variadic templates since they allow us to specify the variable number of base classes.

Here's one simple example that uses the code:

Ex4_13: The Overloaded Pattern. Live code @Compiler Explorer

```
#include <iostream>

template<class... Ts> struct overloaded : Ts... { using Ts::operator()...; };
template<class... Ts> overloaded(Ts...) -> overloaded<Ts...>;

int main() {
    const auto test = overloaded{
        [](const int& i) { std::cout << "int: " << i << '\n'; },
        [](const float& f) { std::cout << "float: " << f << '\n'; },
        [](const std::string& s) { std::cout << "string: " << s << '\n'; }
    };

    test("10.0f");
}
```

In the above example, we create a `test` object which is composed of three lambdas. Then we can call the object with a parameter, and the correct lambda will be selected, depending on the type of the input parameter.

Let's now have a closer look at the core parts of this pattern.

Those two lines of code benefits from three features available since C++17:

- Pack expansions in `using` declarations - short and compact syntax with variadic templates.

- Custom template argument deduction rules - that allows converting a list of lambda objects into a list of base classes for the overloaded class. (note: not needed in C++20!).
- Extension to aggregate initialisation - before C++17 you couldn't aggregate initialise type that derives from other types.

In the C++11 chapter, we already covered the need for using declaration. This is important for bringing the call operators into the same scope of the overloaded structure. In C++17 we got a syntax that supports variadic templates, which was not possible in the previous revisions of the language.

Let's now try to understand the remaining two features:

Custom Template Argument Deduction Rules

We derive from lambdas, and then we expose their operator() as we saw in the previous section. But how can we create objects of this overload type?

As you know, there's no way to know up-front the type of the lambda, as the compiler has to generate some unique type name for each of them. For example, we cannot just write:

```
overload<LambdaType1, LambdaType2> myOverload { ... } // ???
// what is LambdaType1 and LambdaType2 ??
```

The only way that could work would be some make function (as template argument deduction works for function templates since, like, always):

```
template <typename... T>
constexpr auto make_overloader(T&&... t) {
    return overloaded<T...>{std::forward<T>(t)...};
}
```

With template argument deduction rules that were added in C++17, we can simplify the creation of common template types and the make_overloader function is not needed.

For example, for simple types, we can write:

```
std::pair strDouble { std::string{"Hello"}, 10.0 };
// strDouble is std::pair<std::string, double>
```

There's also an option to define custom deduction guides. The Standard library uses a lot of them, for example, for std::array:

```
template <class T, class... U>
array(T, U...) -> array<T, 1 + sizeof...(U)>;
```

and the above rule allows us to write:

```
array test{1, 2, 3, 4, 5};
// test is std::array<int, 5>
```

For the overloaded pattern we can specify a custom deduction guide:

```
template<class... Ts> overloaded(Ts...) -> overloaded<Ts...>;
```

Now, when we initialise an overload with two lambdas:

```
overloaded myOverload { [](int) { }, [](double) { } };
```

The template arguments for overload will be correctly deduced. In our case, the compiler knows the types of the two lambdas so it can resolve the types which the overload inherits from.

 Checkout the C++20 chapter - Updates on page 125 as in the new Standard, the Class Template Argument Deduction is improved! For the overloaded pattern, it means that we don't have to write custom deduction guides!

Let's now go to the last missing part of the puzzle - aggregate initialisation.

Extension to Aggregate Initialisation

This functionality is relatively straightforward: we can now aggregate initialise a type that derives from other types. From the specification dcl.init.aggr[15]:

---

[15]https://timsong-cpp.github.io/cppwp/n4659/dcl.init.aggr

An aggregate is an array or a class with:

- no user-provided, explicit, or inherited constructors
- no private or protected non-static data members
- no virtual functions, and
- no virtual, private, or protected base classes

For example (sample from the spec draft):

Aggregate Initialisation

```
struct base1 { int b1, b2 = 32; };

struct base2 {
  base2() { b3 = 64; }
  int b3;
};

struct derived : base1, base2 {
    int d;
};

derived d1{{1, 2}, {}, 4};
derived d2{{}, {}, 4};
```

The code initializes d1.b1 with 1, d1.b2 with 2, d1.b3 with 64, d1.d with 4. And for the second object we have: d2.b1 with 0, d2.b2 with 32, d2.b3 with 64, d2.d with 4.

In our case, it has a more significant impact. Because for the overload class, without the aggregate initialisation, we'd had to implement the following constructor:

```
struct overloaded : Fs... {
  template <class ...Ts>
  overloaded(Ts&& ...ts) : Fs{std::forward<Ts>(ts)}...
  {}

  // ...
}
```

It's a lot of code to write, and probably it doesn't cover all of the cases like noexcept.

With aggregate initialisation, we "directly" call the constructor of lambda from the base class list, so there's no need to write it and forward arguments to it explicitly.

OK, we covered a lot, but is there any useful example of the overloaded pattern?

It appears it might be convenient for std::variant visitation.

Example with `std::variant` and `std::visit`

Equipped with the knowledge, we can use inheritance and the overloaded pattern for something more practical. Have a look at an example with the visitation of std::variant:

Ex4_14: The Overloaded Pattern with variant and visit. Live code @Compiler Explorer

```
#include <iostream>
#include <variant>

template<class... Ts> struct overloaded : Ts... { using Ts::operator()...; };
template<class... Ts> overloaded(Ts...) -> overloaded<Ts...>;

int main() {
    const auto PrintVisitor = [](const auto& t) { std::cout << t << "\n"; };

    std::variant<int, float, std::string> intFloatString { "Hello" };

    std::visit(PrintVisitor, intFloatString);

    std::visit(overloaded{
        [](int& i) { i *= 2; },
        [](float& f) { f *= 2.0f; },
        [](std::string& s) { s = s + s; }
```

```
    }, intFloatString);

    std::visit(PrintVisitor, intFloatString);
}
```

In the code above we create a variant class that can hold integers, floating-point or string values. Later there's a call to `PrintVisitor` which outputs the current value of the variant. Please notice that thanks to the generic lambda, the visitor can support all types (which have the << operator implemented).

Now, we have another call to `std::visit` that creates a visitor in place, with three different lambda expressions - one for each type. In this artificial example, we want to multiply the value by two, and for strings, it means joining the values together.

Concurrent Execution Using Lambdas

It's easy to show examples where the lambda runs on the same thread as the caller. But how about asynchronous cases? What if you want to call a lambda on a separate thread? What problems might you encounter? Let's review them in this section.

 This section won't be a tutorial on how to write concurrent code in C++, but it aims to show problems that you can encounter with lambdas in asynchronous code. For more information about concurrency in C++, you can consult separate books like Concurrency with Modern C++[16] by Rainer Grimm or C++ Concurrency in Action[17] by Anthony Williams.

Lambdas with `std::thread`

Let's start with `std::thread` which is available since C++11. As you might already know, `std::thread` accepts a callable object in its constructor. It might be a regular function pointer, a function object or a lambda expression. A simple example:

---

[16]https://leanpub.com/concurrencywithmodernc
[17]https://amzn.to/2Zl0M0r

Ex4_15: Passing lambda to a thread. Live code @Coliru

```cpp
#include <iostream>
#include <thread>
#include <vector>
#include <numeric> // for std::iota

int main() {
    const auto printThreadID = [](const char* str) {
        std::cout << str << ": "
                    << std::this_thread::get_id() << " thread id\n";
    };

    std::vector<int> numbers(100);

    std::thread iotaThread([&numbers, &printThreadID](int startArg) {
            std::iota(numbers.begin(), numbers.end(), startArg);
            printThreadID("iota in");
        }, 10
    );

    iotaThread.join();
    printThreadID("printing numbers in");

    for (const auto& num : numbers)
        std::cout << num << ", ";
}
```

In the above sample, we create a single thread with a lambda expression. The `std::thread` class has a flexible constructor, so we can even pass a value for the argument. In our code `10` is passed into the lambda as `startArg`.

The code is simple because we can control the thread execution, and by joining it, we know that the results of the `iota` will be ready before we print them.

The critical thing to remember is that while lambdas make it easy and convenient to create a thread, it's still the asynchronous execution. Closures are not "special" and also vulnerable to all race conditions and blocking.

This is visible in the following example:

Ex4_16: Updating a shared variable by many threads. Live code @Wandbox

```cpp
#include <iostream>
#include <thread>
#include <vector>

int main() {
    int counter = 0;

    const auto maxThreads = std::thread::hardware_concurrency();
    std::vector<std::thread> threads;
    threads.reserve(maxThreads);
    for (size_t tCounter = 0; tCounter < maxThreads; ++tCounter) {
        threads.push_back(std::thread([&counter]() noexcept {
            for (int i = 0; i < 1000; ++i) {
                ++counter;
                --counter;
                ++counter;
                --counter;
            }
        }));
    }

    for (auto& thread : threads)
        thread.join();

    std::cout << counter << '\n';
}
```

In the example, we're creating several threads[18], and each thread performs some computations on the counter variable. The variable is shared among all the threads.

 In C++20 you can use std::jthread which is a thread that joins on destruction and also accepts stop tokens. This new kind of threading object allows more control for the thread execution.

---

[18]std::thread::hardware_concurrency() is a static member function which returns the number of concurrent threads supported by the implementation. Usually, it might be several hardware threads on a given system. On Wandbox it's usually 3, Coliru reports 4.

While you might expect to see 0 as the final value of counter, the result is undefined. One thread can read the value while others might simultaneously write to it, causing the final result to be non-deterministic.

```
0
0
10
-3
```

To fix the issue, as with regular threading scenarios, we should use some sort of a synchronisation mechanism. For this example, we can use atomics as they seem to be the easiest to use.

Ex4_17: Changing value with atomics. Live code @Wandbox

```cpp
#include <iostream>
#include <thread>
#include <vector>

int main() {
    std::atomic<int> counter = 0;

    const auto maxThreads = std::thread::hardware_concurrency();
    std::vector<std::thread> threads;
    threads.reserve(maxThreads);
    for (size_t tCounter = 0; tCounter < maxThreads; ++tCounter) {
        threads.push_back(std::thread([&counter]() noexcept {
            for (int i = 0; i < 1000; ++i) {
                counter.fetch_add(1);
                counter.fetch_sub(1);
                counter.fetch_add(1);
                counter.fetch_sub(1);
            }
        }));
    }

    for (auto& thread : threads)
        thread.join();
```

```
      std::cout << counter.load() << '\n';
}
```

The code above works as expected because increment and decrement operations are now atomic. It means that when `counter` value changes other threads cannot interrupt this action. The synchronisation makes code safer but at a price of the performance. This is, however, a topic for a much longer discussion and a separate book.

 Another option to solve the synchronisation problem is to have a local variable in each thread that is computed. Then, before the thread ends, we could lock and then update the global value. It's also worth adding that defining a variable as `volatile` doesn't provide correct synchronisation. And in C++20 `volatile` is deprecated in many places.

As we can see, it's quite handy to create a thread with a lambda expression. It's local to your executing thread, and you can do everything like with a regular function or function object.

Let's now try another technique that is available in C++.

Lambdas with `std::async`

A second way that you can leverage multithreading is through `std::async`. We got that functionality together with threads in C++11. This is a high-level API that allows you to set up and call computations lazily or fully asynchronously.

Let's convert our example with `iota` into the `async` call:

Ex4_18: Invoking code asynchronously with `std::async`. Live code @Coliru

```cpp
#include <iostream>
#include <future>  // for async and future
#include <vector>
#include <numeric> // for std::iota


int main() {
    const auto printThreadID = [](const char* str) {
        std::cout << str << ": "
                  << std::this_thread::get_id() << " thread id\n";
    };
```

```cpp
std::vector<int> numbers(100);

std::future<void> iotaFuture = std::async(std::launch::async,
[&numbers, startArg = 10, &printThreadID]() {
        std::iota(numbers.begin(), numbers.end(), startArg);
        printThreadID("iota in");
    }
);

iotaFuture.get(); // make sure we get the results...
printThreadID("printing numbers in");
for (const auto& num : numbers)
    std::cout << num << ", ";
}
```

This time rather than threads, we rely on the mechanism of std::future. This is an object which handles the synchronisation and guarantees that the results of the invocation are available when we ask for it through .get().

In our case we schedule the execution of the lambda through std::async, and then we need to call .get() to finish the computations. The .get() member function is blocking.

However the code above is cheating a little, as we're using future<void> and the vector is still passed as the reference captured by lambda. As an alternative you might want to create std::future<std::vector<int>> so that we pass vector through the future mechanism:

```cpp
std::future<std::vector<int>> iotaFuture = std::async(std::launch::async,
                                            [startArg = 10]() {
        std::vector<int> numbers(100);
        std::iota(numbers.begin(), numbers.end(), startArg);
        std::cout << "calling from: "
                    << std::this_thread::get_id() << " thread id\n";
        return numbers;
    }
);

auto vec = iotaFuture.get(); // make sure we get the results...
// ...
```

It seems that over the years `std::async`/`std::future` has earned itself a mixed reputation. It looks like the functionality was a bit too rushed. It works for relatively simple cases but fails with advanced scenarios like:

- continuation,
- task merging,
- no cancellation/joining,
- it's not a regular type,
- and few other issues.

If you want to know more, you should read or watch the following resources:

- There is a Better Future - Felix Petriconi - code::dive 2018 - YouTube[19]
- code::dive 2016 conference – Sean Parent – Better Code: Concurrency - YouTube[20]
- Core C++ 2019 :: Avi Kivity :: Building efficient I/O intensive applications with Seastar - YouTube[21]

Lambdas and Parallel Algorithms from C++17

After discussing the threading support in C++11, we can move to further standards: C++17. This time you have a super easy-to-use technique that allows you to parallelise most of the algorithms from the Standard Library. All you have to do is to specify the first argument into the algorithm, for example:

```
auto myVec = GenerateVector();
std::sort(std::execution::par, myVec.begin(), myVec.end());
```

Please notice the first argument: `std::execution::par`. It's used to enable parallel execution of the sort algorithm.

And we have other options:

---

[19]https://www.youtube.com/watch?v=WZdKFlH7qxo
[20]https://www.youtube.com/watch?v=QIHy8pXbneI
[21]https://www.youtube.com/watch?v=p8d28t4qCTY&feature=emb_logo

Policy Name	Description
sequenced_policy	It is an execution policy type used as a unique type to disambiguate parallel algorithm overloading and require that a parallel algorithm's execution not be parallelised.
parallel_policy	It is an execution policy type used as a unique type to disambiguate parallel algorithm overloading and indicate that a parallel algorithm's execution may be parallelised.
parallel_unsequenced_policy	It is an execution policy type used as a unique type to disambiguate parallel algorithm overloading and indicate that a parallel algorithm's execution may be parallelised and vectorised.

For each policy we have a predefined global instance that you can pass to algorithms:

- std::execution::par

- std::execution::seq

- std::execution::par_unseq

Execution policy declarations and global objects are located in the <execution> header.

 In C++20 there's also one more execution policy: unsequenced_policy along with the global instance std::execution::unseq. It's used to enable vectorised execution on a single thread.

While we can easily enable parallel sorting, we can also quickly write some bad code:

Ex4_19: Copying into vector and dangerous behaviour.

```cpp
#include <iostream>
#include <vector>
#include <numeric>
#include <execution>

int main() {
    std::vector<int> vec(1000);
    std::iota(vec.begin(), vec.end(), 0);
    std::vector<int> output;
    std::for_each(std::execution::par, vec.begin(), vec.end(),
        [&output](int& elem) {
            if (elem % 2 == 0) {
```

```
            output.push_back(elem);
        }
    });

    for (const auto& elem : output)
        std::cout << elem << ", ";
}
```

 The code above doesn't contain any "Live Code" link as it requires a compiler with the parallel algorithm support. This is possible in MSVC (starting with VS 2017) but doesn't work well with any online compiler. You can take the code and then play inside Visual Studio.

Do you see all the issues here?

By passing a lambda to `std::for_each` we need to remember that the execution doesn't happen on a single thread and locally. Several threads might be used here, for example, using a thread pool solution. That's why accessing a shared `output` vector is not the best idea. Not only can it insert elements in a wrong order, but it can even crash if several threads attempt to change the vector at the same time.

We can fix the synchronisation problem by having a mutex and locking it before each call of `push_back`. But is that code still efficient? If the filter condition is straightforward and fast to execute, then you might even get slower performance than the serial version (`seq`).

Not to mention that by running it in parallel, you don't know the order of the copied elements in the output vector.

This section shows only a basic overview of the parallel algorithms, and if you like to see more, please have a look at the following article: Bartek's coding blog: The Amazing Performance of C++17 Parallel Algorithms, is it Possible[22].

Lambdas And Async - Wrap Up

To wrap up: Lambda expressions are convenient when you want to start a thread, invoke asynchronous code through `std::async` or use with parallel algorithms. However, it's essential to keep in mind that closure objects aren't unique regarding the concurrency and all challenges apply here as well.

---

[22]https://www.bfilipek.com/2018/11/parallel-alg-perf.html

Summary

In this chapter, you've seen that C++17 joined two essential elements of C++: `constexpr` with lambdas. Now you can use lambdas in a `constexpr` context! This is a necessary step towards improved metaprogramming support in the language. We'll see that even more in the next chapter about C++20.

Additionally, the C++17 Standard addressed the capturing of the `this` pointer problem. In the new standard, you can capture `this` by a copy to the `*this` object so that the code can be much safer.

We also had a look at some use cases for lambdas: IIFE technique, fold expressions and variadic generic lambdas, deriving from lambda expressions and asynchronous code execution. Thanks to the various features enabled in C++17, we now have much nicer syntax and more straightforward ways to write efficient code.

5. Lambdas in C++20

In February 2020, the ISO Committee finally approved the C++20 Standard during the meeting in Prague and pushed it to the official publication (probably at the end of 2020). The new specification brings a lot of substantial improvements to the language and the Standard Library! Lambda expressions also got a few upgrades.

In this chapter, you'll see:

- What changes in C++20.
- New options to capture the this pointer.
- Template lambdas.
- How to improve generic lambdas with concepts.
- How to use lambdas with constexpr algorithms.
- How to make the overloaded pattern even shorter.

You can see the specification related to lambdas in N4861[1] (the current C++20 draft, post Prague version) and the lambda section: [expr.prim.lambda][2].

---

[1]https://timsong-cpp.github.io/cppwp/n4861/
[2]https://timsong-cpp.github.io/cppwp/n4861/expr.prim.lambda

Lambda Syntax Update

With C++20, we have more changes regarding the syntax of lambda expressions:

- You can now add consteval after the parameter list.
- There's an option to specify the template tail.
- And after the trailing return you can put requires declaration.

And here's an updated syntax diagram:

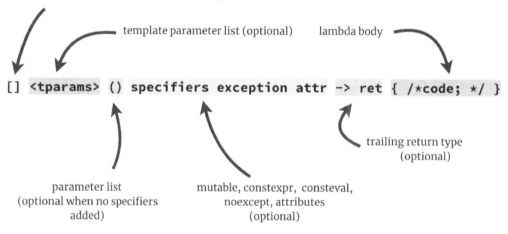

Lambda Syntax in C++20

You can read about new modifications in the next sections.

A Quick Overview of the Changes

With C++20 we'll get the following features related to lambda expressions:

- Allow `[=, this]` as a lambda capture - P0409R2[3] and deprecate implicit capture of this via `[=]` - P0806[4].
- Pack expansion in lambda init-capture: `...args = std::move(args)](){}` - P0780[5].
- `static`, `thread_local`, and lambda capture for structured bindings - P1091[6].
- Template lambdas (also with concepts) - P0428R2[7].
- Simplifying implicit lambda capture - P0588R1[8].
- Default constructible and assignable stateless lambdas - P0624R2[9].
- Lambdas in unevaluated contexts - P0315R4[10].
- `constexpr` Algorithms - most importantly P0202[11],P0879[12] and P1645[13].

If you'd like to know more about C++20, you can have a look at the paper that summarises all the changes: Changes between C++17 and C++20 DIS - P2131[14].

You can also see my Reference Card with all language and the library features: Bartek's coding blog: C++20 Reference Card[15].

Let's now have a quick look at some of the changes.

In most of the cases the newly added features "clean-up" lambda syntax. Plus, C++20 adds enhancements that allow us to use lambdas in advanced scenarios.

For example, with P1091[16] you can capture a structured binding:

---

[3]https://wg21.link/p0409r2
[4]https://wg21.link/P0806
[5]https://wg21.link/P0780
[6]https://wg21.link/P1091
[7]https://wg21.link/P0428R2
[8]https://wg21.link/P0588R1
[9]https://wg21.link/P0624R2
[10]https://wg21.link/P0315R4
[11]https://wg21.link/p0202
[12]https://wg21.link/P0879
[13]https://wg21.link/P1645
[14]https://wg21.link/P2131
[15]https://www.bfilipek.com/2020/01/cpp20refcard.html
[16]https://wg21.link/P1091

Ex5_1: Capturing a structured binding in a lambda. Live code @Wandbox

```cpp
#include <tuple>
#include <string>

auto GetParams() {
    return std::tuple { std::string{"Hello World"}, 42 };
}
int main() {
    auto [x, y] = GetParams();
    const auto ParamLength = [&x, &y]() { return x.length() + y; }();
    return ParamLength;
}
```

 Some compilers supported capturing structured binding even in C++17 (for example GCC), but it was not mandated by the Standard back then.

C++20 also brings clarifications related to *this capture. You'll get a warning if you capture [=] in a method:

Ex5_2: Warning about implicit *this capture. Live code @Wandbox

```cpp
struct Baz {
    auto foo() {
        return [=] { std::cout << s << '\n'; };
    }
    std::string s;
};
```

Compiling with GCC 9 yields the following warning:

```
warning: implicit capture of 'this' via '[=]' is deprecated in C++20
```

The warning appears, because even with [=] you'll capture this as a pointer. It's better to write what you want explicitly: [=, this], or [=, *this].

After a quick review, let's have a look at more prominent features in C++20 related to lambdas.

consteval **Lambdas**

While constexpr from C++11 allows function execution at the compilation phase, it's also possible to run those functions at runtime. It appears that in some cases, it might be best to limit the functionality only to compile-time. That's why in C++20, we have a new keyword that creates functions which conform to the rules of a constexpr function but can be only evaluated at compile-time. Such functions are also called "*immediate functions*".

This new keyword can be also applied to lambdas. Let's review a simple example:

Ex5_3: A Simple Immediate Lambda. Live code @Wandbox

```
int main() {
    const int x = 10;
    auto lam = [](int x) consteval { return x + x; };
    return lam(x);
}
```

Above, you can see that we applied consteval after the argument list of the lambda. This is very similar to the application of constexpr. The critical difference is that if you remove const from x, then the constexpr lambda can work (at runtime), while the immediate lambda won't compile.

By default, if a lambda body follows the rules of a constexpr function, the compiler marks the call operator as constexpr implicitly. This is not the case with consteval as it forms a stronger restriction on such a code. And you cannot use both of those keywords at the same time. You can find the full specification for the new feature in this proposal: P1073R3[17].

Capturing a Parameter Pack

One improvement that we got in C++20 is pack expansion in lambda init-capture.

```
template <typename ...Args> void call(Args&&... args) {
    auto ret = [...capturedArgs = std::move(args)](){};
}
```

[17]http://www.open-std.org/jtc1/sc22/wg21/docs/papers/2018/p1073r3.html

Previously, before C++20, the code wouldn't compile (see the C++11 section on that, page 35) and to work around this issue, you had to wrap arguments into a separate tuple. You can read about the history of this capture restriction in P0780[18].

To sum up, capturing a variadic parameter pack, we can take the example that we got from the C++11 chapter and experiment with it, adding the latest feature. For instance, we can leverage fold expression to do a print of each captured object:

Ex5_4: Capturing a Variadic Pack. Live code @Wandbox

```cpp
#include <iostream>
#include <memory>

template<class First, class... Args>
void captureTest(First&& first, Args&&... args) {
    const auto printer = [first = std::move(first),
                          ...capturedArgs = std::move(args)] {
        std::cout << first;
        ((std::cout << ", " << capturedArgs), ...);
        std::cout << '\n';
    };
    printer();
}

int main() {
    auto ptr = std::make_unique<int>(10);
    captureTest(std::move(ptr), 2, 3, 4);
    captureTest(std::move(ptr), 'a', 'b');
}
```

The output:

```
0x1f0cb20, 2, 3, 4
0, a, b
```

In the example, we used a `printer` object which is similar to the code that we wrote in the C++17 chapter, but this time we capture variables rather than forward them as lambda arguments. The code shows that we can even pass a unique pointer. We pass it twice to the

---

[18]https://wg21.link/P0780

lambda and as you can see the second time we get 0 on the second line since the pointer lost the ownership of the memory block.

Template Lambdas

With C++14, we got generic lambdas which means that parameters declared as `auto` are template parameters.

For a lambda:

```
[](auto x) { x; }
```

The compiler generates a call operator that corresponds to the following template method:

```
template<typename T>
void operator()(T x) { x; }
```

But there was no way to change this template parameter and use "real" template arguments. With C++20 it's possible now.

For example, how can we restrict our lambda to work only with vectors of some type?

We can write a generic lambda:

```
auto foo = [](auto& vec) {
        std::cout<< std::size(vec) << '\n';
        std::cout<< vec.capacity() << '\n';
    };
```

But if you call it with an `int` parameter (like `foo(10);`) then you might get some hard-to-read error:

```
prog.cc: In instantiation of
         'main()::<lambda(const auto:1&)> [with auto:1 = int]':
prog.cc:16:11:    required from here
prog.cc:11:30: error: no matching function for call to 'size(const int&)'
              11 | std::cout<< std::size(vec) << '\n';
```

In C++20 we can write:

```
auto foo = []<typename T>(std::vector<T> const& vec) {
      std::cout<< std::size(vec) << '\n';
      std::cout<< vec.capacity() << '\n';
   };
```

The above lambda resolves to a templated call operator:

```
template <typename T>
void operator()(std::vector<T> const& s) { ... }
```

The template parameter comes after the capture clause [].

If you call it with int (foo(10);) then you get a nicer message:

```
note:    mismatched types 'const std::vector<T>' and 'int'
```

Play with code @Wandbox[19].

In the above example, the compiler can warn us about the mismatch in the interface of the lambda.

Another important aspect is that in the generic lambda example, you only have a variable and not its template type. If you want to access the type, you have to use decltype(x) (for a lambda with (auto x) argument). This makes code more wordy and complicated.

For example (using code from P0428[20]):

---

[19]https://wandbox.org/permlink/gupbJfUfHHQ2y48q
[20]https://wg21.link/P0428

Deducting from generic argument

```cpp
auto f = [](auto const& x) {
    using T = std::decay_t<decltype(x)>;
    T copy = x;
    T::static_function();
    using Iterator = typename T::iterator;
}
```

Can be now written as:

Using template lambda

```cpp
auto f = []<typename T>(T const& x) {
    T copy = x;
    T::static_function();
    using Iterator = typename T::iterator;
}
```

As you can see above, in the first example we need to write:

```cpp
using T = std::decay_t<decltype(x)>;
```

To get the type of the input argument. In the C++20 version, there's no need for this as we can access the template parameter.

And another important use case is perfect forwarding in a generic variadic lambda:

```cpp
// C++17
auto ForwardToTestFunc = [](auto&& ...args) {
  // what's the type of `args` ?
  return TestFunc(std::forward<decltype(args)>(args)...);
};
```

Each time you want to access the type of the template argument, you need to use `decltype()`, but with template lambdas there's no need for that. See below:

```
// C++20:
auto ForwardToTestFunc = []<typename ...T>(T&& ...args) {
  return TestFunc(std::forward<T>(args)...); // we have all the types!
};
```

As you can see, template lambdas provide cleaner syntax and better access to types of arguments.

But there's more! You can also use concepts with lambdas! See in the next section.

Concepts and Lambdas

Concepts are a revolutionary approach for writing templates! They allow you to put constraints on template parameters which improve the readability of code, might speed up compilation time and give better error messages.

One simple example:

A custom concept declaration

```
// define a concept:
template <class T>
concept SignedIntegral = std::is_integral_v<T> && std::is_signed_v<T>;

// use:
template <SignedIntegral T>
void signedIntsOnly(T val) { }
```

In the code above we first create a concept that describes types that are signed and integral. Please notice that we can use existing type traits. Later, we use it to define a template function that supports only types that match the concept. Here we don't use typename T, but we can refer to the name of a concept.

Ok, but how is that related to lambda expressions?

The key part here is the terse syntax and constrained auto template parameter.

Simplifications and Terse Syntax

Thanks to the terse concept syntax you can also write templates without the template<typename..> part.

With unconstrained auto:

```
void myTemplateFunc(auto param) { }
```

Or with constrained auto:

```
void signedIntsOnly(SignedIntegral auto val) { }
void floatsOnly(std::floating_point auto fp) { }
```

Such syntax is similar to what you could use in generic lambdas from C++14, as right now you can also write:

```
void myTemplateFunction(auto val) { }
```

In other words, for lambdas, we can leverage this terse style and for example put extra restrictions on the generic lambda argument:

```
auto GenLambda = [](SignedIntegral auto param) { return param * param + 1; };
```

As you can see in the above example, I restricted the `auto param` with the `SignedIntegral` concept. The whole expression is even more readable than template lambda that we discussed in the previous section.

Here's a bit more complicated example, where we can even define a concept of some class interface:

IRenderable concept, with requires keyword

```
template <typename T>
concept IRenderable = requires(T v) {
    {v.render()} -> std::same_as<void>;
    {v.getVertCount()} -> std::convertible_to<size_t>;
};
```

In the above example we define a concept that matches all types with `render()` and `getVertCount()` member functions. We can then use it to write a generic lambda:

Ex5_5: Implementations of `IRenderable` concept/interface. Live code @Wandbox

```cpp
#include <concepts>
#include <iostream>

template <typename T>
concept IRenderable = requires(T v) {
    {v.render()} -> std::same_as<void>;
    {v.getVertCount()} -> std::convertible_to<size_t>;
};

struct Circle {
    void render() { std::cout << "drawing circle\n"; }
    size_t getVertCount() const { return 10; };
};

struct Square {
    void render() { std::cout << "drawing square\n"; }
    size_t getVertCount() const { return 4; };
};

int main() {
    const auto RenderCaller = [](IRenderable auto &obj) {
        obj.render();
    };
    Circle c;
    RenderCaller(c);
    Square s;
    RenderCaller(s);
}
```

In the above example `RenderCaller` is a generic lambda which can support types that
satisfies the `IRenderable` concept.

Changes to Stateless Lambdas

You might recall from the chapter about C++11 that lambdas, even stateless, are not default
constructible. However, this limitation is lifted in C++20.

That's why, if your lambda doesn't capture anything, then you can write the following code:

Ex5_6: A stateless lambda. Live code @Wandbox

```cpp
#include <set>
#include <string>
#include <iostream>

struct Product {
    std::string name;
    int id {0};
    double price { 0.0};
};

int main() {
    const auto nameCmp = [](const auto& a, const auto& b) {
        return a.name < b.name;
    };
    const std::set<Product, decltype(nameCmp)> prodSet {
        {"Cup", 10, 100.0}, {"Book", 2, 200.5 },
        {"TV set", 1, 2000 }, {"Pencil", 4, 10.5}
    };

    for (const auto &elem : prodSet)
        std::cout << elem.name << '\n';
}
```

In the preceding example, I declared a set that stores a list of Products. I need a way to compare products, so I passed a stateless lambda that compares their string names.

For example, if you compiled that code with a C++17 flag, then you'd get an error about using a deleted default constructor:

```
stl_set.h: In constructor
'std::set<_Key, _Compare, _Alloc>...
[with _Key = Product;
     _Compare = main()::<lambda(const auto:1&, const auto:2&)>;
...
stl_set.h:244:29: error: use of deleted function
'main()::<lambda(const auto:1&, const auto:2&)>::<lambda>()'
```

But in C++20 you can store stateless lambdas and even copy them:

Ex5_7: Storing a stateless lambda. Live code @Wandbox

```
template <typename F>
struct Product {
    int id {0};
    double price { 0.0};
    F predicate;
};

int main() {
    const auto idCmp = [](const auto& a) noexcept {
        return a.id != 0;
    };
    Product p { 10, 10.0, idCmp };
    [[maybe_unused]] auto p2 = p;
}
```

Even more with unevaluated contexts

There are also changes related to advanced use cases like unevaluated contexts. All together with default constructible lambdas you can now write:

```
std::map<int, int, decltype([](int x, int y) { return x > y; })> map;
```

As you can see, it's now possible to specify the lambda inside the declaration of map container. It can be used as a comparator callable type. Such "unevaluated contexts" are especially handy for advanced template metaprogramming. For example, in the proposal of the feature, the authors mention sorting of tuple objects at compile time using a predicate which is a lambda.

More reasoning in P0315R2[21].

Lambdas and `constexpr` Algorithms

If you recall from the previous chapter, since C++17 we can use lambdas which are `constexpr`. With this functionality, you can pass a lambda to functions which are evaluated at compile time. In C++20 most of the standard algorithms are now marked with the `constexpr` keyword which makes `constexpr` lambdas even more convenient!

Let's consider a few examples.

Below you can find code that runs `std::accumulate` on an array, with a custom lambda:

Ex5_8: Using **`std::accumulate`** with a custom **`constexpr`** lambda. Live code @Compiler Explorer

```cpp
#include <array>
#include <numeric>

int main() {
    constexpr std::array arr{ 1, 2, 3, 4, 5, 6, 7, 8, 9, 10 };

    // with constexpr lambda
    static_assert(std::accumulate(begin(arr), end(arr), 0,
        [](auto a, auto b) noexcept {
            return a + b;
        }) == 55);
    return arr[0];
}
```

In the example with `std::accumulate` we used lambda, which is, in fact, the `std::plus` operation.

And in the next example there's a `constexpr` function that takes a `cmp` comparator/predicate for the `count_if` algorithm:

---

[21]https://wg21.link/P0315R2

Ex5_9: Passing a `constexpr` lambda to a custom function. Live code @Compiler Explorer

```cpp
#include <array>
#include <algorithm>

constexpr auto CountValues(auto container, auto cmp) {
    return std::count_if(begin(container), end(container), cmp);
}

int main() {
    constexpr auto minVal = CountValues(std::array{-10, 6, 8, 4, -5, 2, 4, 6 },
        [](auto a) { return a >= 0; }
    );
    return minVal;
}
```

 What standard algorithms are `constexpr`? All of the algorithms from the `<algorithm>`, `<utility>` and `<numeric>`headers are now marked with `constexpr` except of functions `shuffle`, `sample`, `stable_sort`, `stable_-partition`, `inplace_merge` and functions or overloads that accepts the Execution Policy argument. Read more in Papers P0202[22], P0879[23] and P1645[24].

C++20 Updates to the Overloaded Pattern

In the previous chapter, you learned about deriving from multiple lambda expressions and exposing them through the `overloaded` pattern. Such a technique is handy for `std::variant` visitation.

Thanks to the Class Template Argument Deduction (CTAD) updates in C++20 we can now have even shorter syntax!

Why?

It's because in C++20 there are extensions to CTAD and aggregates are automatically handled. That means that there's no need to write a custom deduction guide.

For a simple type:

---

[22]https://wg21.link/p0202
[23]https://wg21.link/P0879
[24]https://wg21.link/P1645

```
template <typename T, typename U, typename V>
struct Triple { T t; U u; V v; };
```

In C++20 you can write:

```
Triple ttt{ 10.0f, 90, std::string{"hello"}};
```

And T will be deduced as float, U as int and V as std::string.

The overloaded pattern in C++20 is now just:

```
template<class... Ts> struct overload : Ts... { using Ts::operator()...; };
```

The proposal for this feature is available in P1021[25] and also P1816[26] (wording).

 GCC10 seems to implement this proposal, but it doesn't work for advanced cases with inheritance, so we have to wait for the full conformance here.

Summary

In this chapter, we reviewed the changes that C++20 has brought.

First of all, we have a few clarifications and improvements: for example with the capture of this, capturing structured bindings or the ability to default construct stateless lambdas. What's more, there are more significant additions! One of the prominent capabilities now is template lambdas and concepts - so that you get more control over generic lambdas.

To sum up, with C++20 and all of its features, lambdas are even more powerful tools!

---

[25]https://wg21.link/P1021
[26]https://wg21.link/P1816

Appendix A - List of Techniques

Below you can find a list of techniques and patterns used throughout the book:

C++11 Chapter

- Calculating the number of invocations - An example of instrumenting a default function object to gather extra information. Starting from page 27.
- Deriving from lambda - A basic technique that allows you to wrap a closure type and extend it with additional functionality. Starting from page 45.
- IIFE - Immediately Invoked Function Expression - An efficient way to compute the value of a `const` variable which requires a complex initialisation without creating an extra function. Starting from page 42.
- Passing a captureless lambda as a function pointer to C-style API functions. Starting from page 39.
- How to store lambdas in a container - we can do a little trick and store lambdas wrapped into `std::function`. Starting from page 49.

C++14 Chapter

- Replacing `std::bind1st`, `std::bind2nd` - how to use Modern C++ and replace deprecated functionality. On page 67.
- An optimisation thanks to capture with initialiser - An example of storing a temporary value used for the body of the lambda. Starting from page 58.
- Perfect forwarding with generic lambdas - How to use `std::forward` on a generic argument to pass the arguments further in the call stack. Starting from page 63.
- LIFTING with lambdas - This allows passing a set of function overloads into a function template which takes a callable object. For example, when you call algorithms from the Standard Library.Starting from page 70.
- Recursive lambdas - Several tricks you can use to call the closure object inside its body. Starting from page 73.
- Variadic generic lambdas - How to use variadic arguments in a lambda expression. Starting from page 62.

C++17 Chapter

- The overload pattern - The mechanism that allows to derive from multiple lambda expressions and pass it to `std::visit`. Starting from page 93.

- IIFE improvements - How to improve readability with `std::invoke`. Starting from page 87.

- Extracting Functions with IIFE - interesting exercise where you can use IIFE to wrap the code and then gradually convert that into a separate smaller function. Starting from page 88.

- Updates to Variadic Generic Lambdas - Leveraging fold expressions for simpler code. Starting from page 91.

- Lambdas and asynchronous execution - What are the pitfalls of using lambdas with threads async and parallel algorithms. Starting from page 99.

C++20 Chapter

- Updates to the overloaded pattern - More simplification with extended class template deduction guides. Starting from page 124.

- Updates to Capturing a Parameter Pack - Better support for r-value references. Starting from page 113.

- Lambdas and `constexpr` Algorithms - C++20 brings a lot of `constexpr` standard algorithms and thanks to constexpr `lambdas` you can write short code. Starting from page 123.

Appendix B - Six Advantages of C++ Lambda Expressions[27]

I hope you enjoyed the book and learned a lot about lambda expressions. This powerful feature has become one of the most visible trademarks of Modern C++. The evolution of lambdas is also tightly coupled with improvements in the language, and thus by reading this book, you've also seen a lot of cool C++ techniques where lambdas make things simpler and more readable.

As a summary of the book, let's wrap up our knowledge and list a few lambdas' benefits.

1. Lambdas Make Code More Readable

The first point might sound quite obvious, but it's always good to appreciate the fact that since C++11, we've been able to write more compact code.

For example, in the chapter about C++98/03 we tried to decipher the following code that used bind expressions and predefined helper function objects from the Standard Library:

Ex6_1: Functional Composition and `std::bind`. Live code @Compiler Explorer

```cpp
#include <algorithm>
#include <functional>
#include <vector>

int main() {
    using std::placeholders::_1;
    const std::vector<int> v { 1, 2, 3, 4, 5, 6, 7, 8, 9 };
    const auto val = std::count_if(v.begin(), v.end(),
                            std::bind(std::logical_and<bool>(),
                            std::bind(std::greater<int>(),_1, 2),
                            std::bind(std::less_equal<int>(),_1,6)));
    return val;
}
```

---

[27]this appendix is an extended blog article available at https://www.bfilipek.com/2020/05/lambdasadvantages.html

Can you immediately tell what the final value of val is?

Let's now rewrite this into lambda expression:

Ex6_2: Cleaner Syntax with Lambdas. Live code @Compiler Explorer

```cpp
#include <algorithm>
#include <vector>

int main() {
    const std::vector<int> v { 1, 2, 3, 4, 5, 6, 7, 8, 9 };
    const auto val = std::count_if(v.begin(), v.end(),
                        [](int v) noexcept { return v > 2 && v <= 6;});
    return val;
}
```

Isn't that better?

Not only have we got shorter syntax for the anonymous function object, but we could even reduce one include statement (as there's no need for <functional> any more).

In C++98/03, it was convenient to use predefined helpers to build those callable objects on the fly. They were handy and even allowed you to compose functionalities to get some complex conditions or operations. However, the main issue is the hard-to-learn syntax. You can of course still use them, even with C++17 or C++20 code (and for places where the use of lambdas is not possible), but I guess that their application for complex scenarios is a bit limited now. In most cases, it's far easier to use lambdas.

I bet you can list many examples from your projects where applying lambda expressions made code much cleaner and easier to read.

2. Lambdas Can Compile 7x Faster than `std::bind`!

Let's have a look at the following code:

```cpp
int sum3(int a, int b, int c) {
    return a + b + c;
}

int main() {
    int x = 10;
    auto sum2 = [x](int a, int b) { return sum3(x, a, b);}};
    return sum2(10, 10);
}
```

And the second one, using `std::bind`:

```cpp
#include <functional>

int sum3(int a, int b, int c) {
    return a + b + c;
}

int main() {
    int x = 10;
    auto sum2 = std::bind(sum3, std::placeholders::_1,
                          std::placeholders::_2, x);
    return sum2(10, 10);
}
```

Do you know which one is faster to compile?

We can compare the speed using build-bench (an online benchmarking compiler), here's the link to our experiment: lambdas vs `std::bind` @BuildBench[28].

The results?

---

[28]https://build-bench.com/b/S7L7U0jNHQpgifhcKq_ZMudZmow

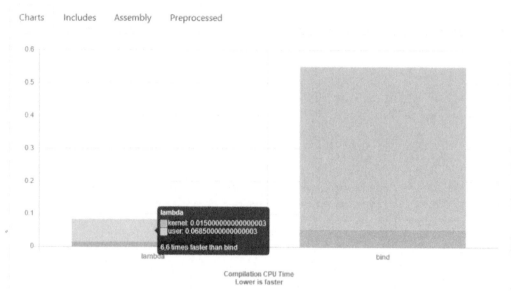

Compilation time

Lambdas are almost 7x times faster to compile than `std::bind` (it's using GCC 10.1, the C++20 mode, and the optimisation -O3 level)

Version	Compilation Normalised CPU Time
With `std::bind`	0.4955
Width a lambda	0.0685

Why is that? It's mainly because there's no need to include headers. The version with `std::bind` results in 40890 lines of code! Compared to just 16 lines of code for the lambda version! Not surprisingly the compiler does a great job as the final assembler is the same amount of lines. It also means that it should give us the same runtime performance.

Here are other experiments with some more realistic scenarios (when we include some other types from the Standard Library):

- With `std::cout` @BuildBench[29] - now it's 40% faster (see `Ex6_3`),
- With extra algorithms @BuildBench[30] - only 10% faster (see `Ex6_4`).

Since lambda expressions are a pure language feature, then the compiler has a much simpler job, and the resulting C++ code is much smaller. It might not give us better runtime

---

[29]https://build-bench.com/b/CgjIf0axxeVEMEYpgH5bB2rUvEk
[30]https://build-bench.com/b/VGmSdXBSv6MYn4P5MWbSIYQwCbw

performance (because compilers can optimise a lot of library code and make it inline), but they result in a cleaner code.

3. Lambdas Improve Locality of the Code

In C++98/03, you had to create functions or custom function objects that could be distant from where you passed them as callable objects.

This is hard to show on simple artificial examples, but you can imagine a large source file, with more than a thousand lines of code. The code organisation might cause function objects types to be located in one section of a file (for example on top). The use of a function object could be hundreds of lines further or earlier in the code. If you wanted to see a particular function object's definition, you had to navigate to a completely different place in the file. Such jumping might slow your productivity.

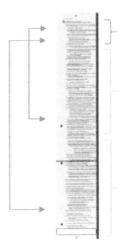

Jumping around a source file

We should also add one more topic to the first and the second point. Lambdas improve locality, readability, but there's also **the naming part**. Since lambdas are anonymous, there's no need for you to select the meaningful name for all of your small functions or function objects.

4. Lambdas Allow Storing State Easily

In the C++11 chapter, we covered a simple example of modifying the default comparator for `std::sort` so that we could count the number of invocations.

Ex6_5: Capturing state. Live code @Compiler Explorer

```cpp
#include <algorithm>
#include <iostream>
#include <vector>

int main() {
    std::vector<int> vec { 0, 5, 2, 9, 7, 6, 1, 3, 4, 8 };

    size_t compCounter = 0;
    std::sort(vec.begin(), vec.end(),
        [&compCounter](int a, int b) noexcept {
            ++compCounter;
            return a < b;
        });

    std::cout << "number of comparisons: " << compCounter << '\n';

    for (const auto& v : vec)
        std::cout << v << ", ";
}
```

As you can see, we can capture a local variable and then use it across all invocations of the binary comparator. Such behaviour is not possible with regular functions[31], but it's also not straightforward with custom function object types. Lambdas make it very natural and also very convenient to use.

5. Lambdas Allow Several Overloads in the Same Place

This is one of the coolest examples related to lambdas and several major Modern C++ features (primarily available in C++17). We learned about this technique in the C++17 chapter, where

---

[31]You can use globals or static variables in a regular function, but it's not the best solution.

we discussed the ability to inherit from several lambdas.

Have a look:

Ex6_6: The overloaded Pattern. Live code @Compiler Explorer

```cpp
#include <iostream>
#include <string>
#include <variant>

template<class... Ts> struct overload : Ts... { using Ts::operator()...; };
template<class... Ts> overload(Ts...) -> overload<Ts...>;

int main() {
    std::variant<int, float, std::string> intFloatString { "Hello" };
    std::visit(overload  {
        [](const int& i) { std::cout << "int: " << i; },
        [](const float& f) { std::cout << "float: " << f; },
        [](const std::string& s) { std::cout << "string: " << s; }
      },
      intFloatString
    );
}
```

The above example is a handy approach to building a callable object with all possible overloads for variant types on the fly. The overloaded pattern is conceptually equivalent to the following structure:

The Print Visitor Structure

```cpp
struct PrintVisitor {
  void operator()(int& i) const { cout << "int: " << i; }
  void operator()(float& f) const { cout << "float: " << f; }
  void operator()(const std::string& s) const { cout << "str: " << s; }
};
```

Additionally, it's also possible to write a compact generic lambda that works for all types from a variant object. This can support runtime polymorphism based on std::variant.

Ex6_7: Runtime Polymorphism Based on std::variant/std::visit. Live code @Compiler Explorer

```
#include <variant>

struct Circle { void Draw() const { } };
struct Square { void Draw() const { } };
struct Triangle { void Draw() const { } };

int main() {
    std::variant<Circle, Square, Triangle> shape;
    shape = Triangle{};
    const auto callDraw = [](auto& sh) { sh.Draw(); };
    std::visit(callDraw, shape);
}
```

This technique is an alternative to runtime polymorphism based on virtual functions. Here we can work with unrelated types. There's no need for a common base class. You can read about this approach in my blog article Runtime Polymorphism with `std::variant` and `std::visit`[32].

6. Lambdas Get Better with Each Revision of C++!

The initial version of lambdas in C++11 had some limitations, but then with each new C++ Standard those issues were fixed and new features added.

Here's the list of major changes related to lambdas that we got with C++ Standards (after C++11):

C++14

- Default parameters - this is a small feature but makes lambdas similar to regular functions.

- Generic lambdas - you can pass `auto` argument, and then the compiler expands this code into a function template.

  - Such flexibility allows for tricks like recursive lambdas

---

[32]https://www.bfilipek.com/2020/04/variant-virtual-polymorphism.html

- Capture with initialiser - with this feature you can capture not only existing variables from the outer scope, but also create new state variables for lambdas.
  - This feature allows us to capture moveable only types or be more explicit about capturing data members.
  - Variadic generic arguments are also possible!
- Common specification for auto return type deduction for regular functions and lambdas.

C++17

- `constexpr` lambdas - in C++17 your lambdas can work in a `constexpr` context.
- Capturing `this` improvements - Before C++17 `this` pointer was captured only as a pointer, leading to dangling issues. In C++17 you can capture a copy of the object represented by `this*`.
- Fold Expressions that can improve generic variadic lambdas.
- `std::invoke` a new addition from The Standard Library makes IIFE expression more readable.
- Class Template Argument Deduction and Extensions to Aggregate Initialisation make it possible to implement the overloaded pattern.

C++20

- Template lambdas - improvements to generic lambdas which offer more control over the input template argument.
- Lambdas and concepts - Lambdas can also work with constrained auto and Concepts, so they are as flexible as function objects and function templates.
- Lambdas in unevaluated contexts - you can now create a map or a set and use a lambda as a predicate.
- You can now capture a structured binding.
- Lambdas can be marked as `consteval` so that they are evaluated only at compile time.
- There's a nicer syntax to capturing a Parameter Pack.
- Stateless lambdas are default constructible and assignable.

References

C++ Standard Drafts

Here are final drafts of C++ Standards, usually with editorial fixes. Available and hosted at timsong-cpp/cppwp[33].

Sections on Lambda Expression:

- C++11 N3337 - [expr.prim.lambda][34]
- C++14 N4140 - [expr.prim.lambda][35]
- C++17 N4659 - [expr.prim.lambda][36]
- C++20 N4861 - [expr.prim.lambda][37]

Other

- Lambda expressions - cppreference.com[38]
- C++ compiler support - cppreference.com[39]
- Value categories - cppreference.com[40]
- Effective Modern C++: 42 Specific Ways to Improve Your Use of C++11 and C++14 1st Edition by Scott Meyers, see @Amazon.com[41]
- Functional Programming in C++: How to improve your C++ programs using functional techniques by Ivan Cukic, see @Amazon[42]
- Microsoft Docs - Lambda Expressions in C++[43]

[33]https://github.com/timsong-cpp/cppwp
[34]https://timsong-cpp.github.io/cppwp/n3337/expr.prim.lambda
[35]https://timsong-cpp.github.io/cppwp/n4140/expr.prim.lambda
[36]https://timsong-cpp.github.io/cppwp/n4659/expr.prim.lambda
[37]https://timsong-cpp.github.io/cppwp/n4861/expr.prim.lambda
[38]https://en.cppreference.com/w/cpp/language/lambda
[39]https://en.cppreference.com/w/cpp/compiler_support
[40]https://en.cppreference.com/w/cpp/language/value_category
[41]https://amzn.to/2ZpA7yz
[42]https://amzn.to/3oEMVMY
[43]https://docs.microsoft.com/en-us/cpp/cpp/lambda-expressions-in-cpp?view=vs-2017

- Sticky Bits - Demystifying C++ lambdas[44]

- The View from Aristeia - Lambdas vs. Closures[45]

- Sy Brand - Passing overload sets to functions[46]

- Jason Turner - C++ Weekly - Ep 128 - C++20's Template Syntax For Lambdas[47]

- Jason Turner - C++ Weekly - Ep 41 - C++17's constexpr Lambda Support[48]

- Stack Overflow - c++ - Recursive lambda functions in C++11[49]

- Pedro Melendez - Recursive lambdas in C++(14)[50]

- Andreas Fertig - Under the covers of C++ lambdas - Part 2: Captures, captures, captures[51]

- Scott Meyers - Standard C++ - Universal References in C++11[52]

- Standard C++ Website - Quick Q: Why can noexcept generate faster code than throw()?[53]

- Bjarne Stroustrup - C++ Style and Technique FAQ[54]

- C++ Core Guidelines[55]

- Jonathan Boccara - How Lambdas Make Function Extraction Safer - Fluent C++[56]

[44]https://blog.feabhas.com/2014/03/demystifying-c-lambdas/
[45]http://scottmeyers.blogspot.com/2013/05/lambdas-vs-closures.html
[46]https://blog.tartanllama.xyz/passing-overload-sets/
[47]https://www.youtube.com/watch?v=ixGiE4-1GA8&
[48]https://www.youtube.com/watch?v=kmza9U_niq4
[49]https://stackoverflow.com/questions/2067988/recursive-lambda-functions-in-c11
[50]http://pedromelendez.com/blog/2015/07/16/recursive-lambdas-in-c14/
[51]https://andreasfertig.blog/2020/11/under-the-covers-of-cpp-lambdas-part-2-captures-captures-captures/
[52]https://isocpp.org/blog/2012/11/universal-references-in-c11-scott-meyers
[53]https://isocpp.org/blog/2014/09/noexcept-optimization
[54]https://stroustrup.com/bs_faq2.html
[55]https://isocpp.github.io/CppCoreGuidelines/CppCoreGuidelines
[56]https://www.fluentcpp.com/2020/11/13/how-lambdas-make-function-extraction-safer/

Index

Printed in Great Britain
by Amazon

26523673R00090